RADICAL ISLAM

WHAT YOU NEED TO KNOW

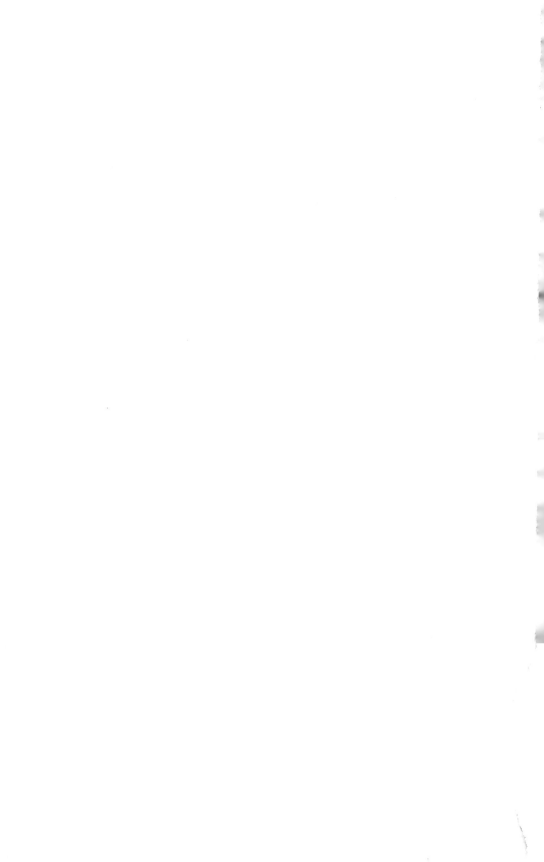

JIM DENISON

RADICAL ISLAM

WHAT YOU NEED TO KNOW

WHY DO THEY STILL HATE US?
WAS BIN LADEN'S DEATH JUST?
SPIRITUAL IMPLICATIONS OF THE WAR ON TERROR

Radical Islam: What You Need to Know.

Library of Congress Cataloging-in-Publication Data
Pending

Printed in Canada
14 13 12 11 10 09 08
7 6 5 4 3 2 1

DEDICATION

To Janet,
My greatest love and best friend

To Ryan and Craig,
Our greatest gifts

To Candice and Rachel,
Welcome.

ACKNOWLEDGEMENTS

This is the hardest and easiest book I've ever written. Hardest, because it deals with the greatest challenge our civilization faces. Easiest, because I wrote the book alongside the best ministry partners I've ever known.

Jeff Byrd co-founded the Denison Forum on Truth and Culture with me more than two years ago and has been my best friend and colleague for 23 years. Brittany Kulick is our brilliant and gifted media leader and the hands-on coordinator of this project. Minni Elkins is my long-time associate and one of the most godly people I've ever known. Scott Rosa is our remarkable, servant-hearted Information Technology leader and my dear friend. Billie Byrd is our administrative leader and one of the most enthusiastic people I've ever met. Mark Cook and Ryan Denison, our research interns, contributed valuable data and wise counsel. Dani Crawford and Morgan Byrd, our summer interns, have made my library and our office both efficient and effective.

Karl Schaller and the team at The Elevation Group have been a joy and delight. Their support and guidance have shepherded this project well. And Tom Neven gave remarkable insight and editorial assistance before returning to duty in Afghanistan. I pray for Tom and his family daily, with gratitude.

Most of all, this book would not be possible without the inspiration and encouragement of my wife and our sons. Janet is the wisest and most godly person I know. Her support across 31 years of marriage continues to amaze and bless me. And Ryan and Craig are the godliest young men any father could know. They are God's greatest gifts to me. It is a daily privilege to serve the King and his Kingdom with them.

CONTENTS

FOREWORD

At age 15 I was ready to die for my religion of Islam. Born and raised in a devout Muslim home in South Asia, I was trained to become an Islamic leader—but God had other plans. One night as a young man I dreamed I was burning in a lake of fire, and that began my quest for the true God, a journey that led me to the feet of Jesus.

Setting foot on American soil for the first time as a young adult, I had never met a Christian, never seen a church, and never really knew what a genuine American/Christian—for me these terms were synonymous at the time—was like, only the propaganda I had learned in the *madrassas* (Islamic schools).

The events of 9/11 are still painfully raw for many. Ten years later questions remain about the world's fastest growing religion and the world-view of its 1.6 billion adherents. While not all Muslims are terrorists, the threat of radical Islam is a real and serious issue the next generation will have to face.

The copy of Dr. Jim Denison's book that you now hold provides a timely, insightful interpretation of this movement in our times. I find Dr. Denison's understanding of radical Islam to be accurate and balanced. His intellectual brilliance and excellent communication skills engage and support readers in navigating these complex issues.

Not only is Jim a brilliant scholar, but he also has first-hand experience working with Muslims in East Malaysia and in my native country of Bangladesh, the third largest Islamic nation in the world. I have seen his compassion for Muslims as we ministered together, sitting on the concrete floor of a village mosque and *madrassa* in dialogue with imams, *madrassa* teachers, and children who were memorizing the entire Qur'an—such *madrassas* that serve as potential breeding grounds for terrorism.

Dr. Denison is a dear friend, and it has been a privilege to sit under him as my pastor for more than 10 years at Park Cities Baptist Church in Dallas. He is a sought-after speaker and prolific writer; we have been honored and blessed to hear his remarkable teaching on radical Islam at our Gospel For Muslims annual Muslim Background Believer's Conference.

I pray *Radical Islam* reaches the hands and hearts of Jesus' followers across America and the globe. Dr. Denison's work will equip us to better understand our post-9/11 world and the role of radical Islam, helping us to fight terrorism with the love and hope that Jesus brings.

Dr. Abraham Sarker
Founder and President, Gospel For Muslims

THE GREATEST THREAT WE'VE EVER FACED

On September 11, 2011, Ground Zero will be open to the public for the first time in ten years.

The roof of Tower One, often called the Freedom Tower, will eventually stand 1,368 feet tall, the same height as the original One World Trade Center. With its spire added, it will stand 1,776 feet tall, symbolic of the year of our independence.

Tower Two is expected to reach a height of 1,350 feet; Tower Three will stand 1,255 feet high; and Tower Four is planned for a height of 946 feet. Hundreds of trees have been planted across the 16-acre site. Two memorial pools will mark the footprints of World Trade Center Tower One and Tower Two. The National September 11 Memorial and Museum opens on the 10th anniversary of the worst terrorism attack in our nation's history.

RADICAL ISLAM

I made my first visit to the World Trade Center several years before 9/11. Standing on the sidewalk, I tried to see the tops of the Twin Towers, but failed. If I had lain on the ground I still couldn't have seen them—they were that tall.

Last year I returned to Ground Zero for the first time since 9/11. I stood at the site and remembered that horrific day. Staring into the morning skies, my mind flashed back to television images of skyscrapers burning and people jumping to their deaths. Then the towers collapsed to the ground in a hideous cloud of debris and dust. Looking back over the 10 years since that shocking morning, it seemed that the nation we were before the War on Terror had vanished with them.

The statistics alone are staggering:

- 2,750 died in the World Trade Center, including 343 firefighters and paramedics, 23 New York City police officers, and 37 Port Authority officers. Ten thousand others have been treated for injuries.
- Only six people who were in the towers at the time of the attacks survived.
- When the Pentagon was attacked, 125 military personnel were killed, along with 64 airplane passengers.
- Forty-five died aboard United Flight 93.[1]

Since 9/11, terrorism attacks around the world have continued unabated. In 2002, a bombing in Bali, Indonesia, killed 202 people from 21 countries and injured 240. In 2003, a suicide bomber in Tel Aviv, Israel, killed three and injured more than 50. Later that year, 14 bombers in Casablanca, Morocco, killed 33 and injured 100. Still later that year, bombings in Istanbul, Turkey, killed 50 and injured 700. In 2004, explosions in three Madrid train stations killed 170 and injured 500. In 2005, explosions in

London's transportation network killed 37 and injured 700. In 2010, terrorists attacking a train in Moscow killed 39 and injured 71. All these deaths can be directly attributed to the teachings of radical Islam.

Meanwhile, the costs of fighting the War on Terror continue to escalate. As of June 6, 2011, 6,043 American troops had died in Iraq and Afghanistan and 43,964 had been injured. Estimates regarding Iraqi and Afghan casualties range from 150,000 (80 percent civilians)[2] to more than a million.[3]

At this writing, the United States has spent more than $1.283 trillion on the war effort. This is nearly the amount we spent on Vietnam ($738 billion), Korea ($341 billion) and World War I ($334 billion) combined (all figures in today's dollars). It is estimated that we may spend another $600 billion in medical care for injured military personnel.[4]

In the 10 years since 9/11, *Time* magazine devoted 13 cover stories to terrorism issues. *The New York Times* published 70,831 stories on terrorism-related subjects. Can you think of any issue that has dominated our news over the last decade more than radical Islam?

Here's my point: After 10 years, multiplied thousands of deaths and injuries, and trillions of dollars spent, most Americans still don't know why our enemy hates us. Stop people on the street and ask them why we fought World War II; if they know history at all they'll be able to answer your question quickly. We knew that we were fighting Communist expansion in Korea and Vietnam and that we were defending Kuwait and Saudi Arabia from Saddam Hussein in Operation DESERT STORM.

But ask Americans why terrorists flew three planes into buildings and attempted a fourth attack on that terrible day 10 years ago. "Because they hate us," they'll say. If you ask them why they hate us, they don't know.

This book is written to answer that question.

I am convinced that radical Islam constitutes the greatest threat the West has ever faced. It is imperative that we understand our enemy—who they are, what they believe, and how to defeat them. Otherwise, the next 10 years will be harder than the last 10.

The good news is that this is a war we can win. The bad news is that if we don't, 9/11 will have destroyed more than the Twin Towers. Our values and way of life are at stake, more than ever before in our history. Let's learn why and what you can do about it today.

June 2011
Dallas, Texas

ENDNOTES

1. http://www.history.com/topics/9-11-attacks, accessed June 11, 2011
2. http://en.wikipedia.org/wiki/Iraq_War_documents_leak#cite_note-53, accessed June 11, 2011.
3. http://www.opinion.co.uk/Newsroom_details.aspx?NewsId=120, accessed June 11, 2011.
4. http://news.bbc.co.uk/2/hi/7304300.stm, accessed June 11, 2011.

CHAPTER ONE

WHO WAS USAMA BIN LADEN?[1] WAS HIS DEATH JUST?

America's "most wanted" fugitive looks eerily like me. Glen Stewart Godwin was born a month after I was. We're both 6 feet tall with medium build, dark hair and green eyes. That's where the similarities end. Godwin escaped from Folsom Prison in 1987, where he was serving a sentence for murder; he was later arrested and imprisoned in Guadalajara, where he escaped again.

He is joined on the FBI's "Most Wanted" list[2] by Jason Derek Brown, an avid golfer who speaks fluent French, holds a Master's Degree in International Business, and allegedly killed an armored car guard outside a movie theater and then fled with the money. Other members of his infamous fraternity include a Russian mobster, a kidnapper, a man who murdered his wife and children, and until May 2, 2011, Usama bin Laden.

The FBI's website describes bin Laden as "the leader of a terrorist organization known as al-Qaeda, 'The Base.' He is left-handed and walks with a cane." Unlike Glen Godwin and most of his fellow fugitives, whose rewards are $100,000 each, the bounty on bin Laden was $25 million. Who was he? Why was he such a threat to our nation? How did he die? Was his death just?[3]

If the Vanderbilts were Arabs

Cornelius Vanderbilt was the fourth of nine children born to a modest family on Staten Island. He left school in 1805 at age 11 and built a railroad and shipping empire that made him one of the world's wealthiest men.

Mohamed bin Laden[4] was Saudi Arabia's version of the Vanderbilt success story. The future father of Usama bin Laden and 53 other children was born in 1908 in Yemen. The region, known as Hadramout, is famous for towering mud-brick structures and the engineers who built them. It is one of the most ancient places on earth, tracing its lineage to Seba, the grandson of Ham and son of Cush (Genesis 10:7) who founded the Sabeans, the ancestors of modern-day Yemen.

Mohamed Bin Laden's father died when he was still a child. He soon joined a camel caravan and walked to the port city of Mukalla, sailed to Africa, and found work in Ethiopia. There his right eye was damaged—some reports claim the injury was an accident, while others blame a teacher's blow—so that he wore a glass eye for the rest of his life.

He eventually made his way to Jeddah, an ancient city beside the Red Sea that serves as the gateway to Mecca. Hundreds of thousands of Muslims come through the city every year on the Hajj, the pilgrimage to Islam's holiest city. Mohamed got a job working for pilgrims as a porter, then sold fruit from a donkey.

He soon found a job as a builder, and was successful enough to found his own small company in 1931. He was not tall (he stood 5 feet, 8 inches), could barely read and never learned to write, but he was a natural leader and excellent organizer. He could do complicated math in his head and was brilliant with finances. His company found work in small construction projects, and then fortune intervened.

Abdulaziz ibn Saud founded the modern nation of Saudi Arabia in 1932. About this time oil was discovered on the Arabian Peninsula. The Arabian American Oil Company, or Aramco, was formed to develop the finds. Mohamed bin Laden was soon employed by Aramco as a mason and bricklayer. His excellent work came to the attention of the royal family, who invited him to begin working on their palaces.

No one knows exactly how bin Laden first met ibn Saud, the King of Saudi Arabia, but the two formed a partnership that revolutionized the nation. Bin Laden's company was employed to build mosques, then a series of dams and reservoirs to supply water to Mecca. When bin Laden paved the 350-mile road from the port city of Jeddah to Medina, Islam's second-holiest city, his national reputation was secured.

Over time, bin Laden's construction company would rebuild the tourist sites of Mecca and Medina, as well as the Temple Mount in Jerusalem and every major road in the Kingdom. He became the largest customer of Caterpillar dirt-moving equipment on the planet. His company became the richest in Saudi Arabia, growing to more than $5 billion in assets and employing more than 35,000 people; his was known as the wealthiest non-royal family in the kingdom.

Mohamed bin Laden soon branched out into telecommunications, engineering, concrete, and consulting. His operations sold soft drinks, built the Kuala Lumpur airport, and partnered with such firms as General Electric and Citigroup. Many members of his family moved to homes in the West. (On September 11, 2001, 12 lived in the Boston area alone.)

Bin Laden was famous for his charity, on one occasion paying for surgery in Spain for a man who had lost his sight, on another occasion building a well and mosque for a village in need. Following his lead, his family has since contributed large sums to endow fellowships at Harvard, Oxford and Tufts.

He married 22 times, though he was never married to more than four wives at a time (thus following Islamic law). He fathered at least 54 children; the 17th was named "Usama." Mohamed bin Laden died on September 3, 1967 when his airplane, piloted by an American, crashed and burned.

"A shy kid, very nice, very considerate"

Usama bin Laden was born in Riyadh, Saudi Arabia on March 10, 1957, the only child of his mother, Alia Ghanem, and his father. He was the seventh son of his father. Usama means "the Lion" and was the name of one of the Prophet Muhammad's companions. His mother was about 15 when he was born.

Shortly after their divorce, his father arranged for her to marry an employee named Muhammad al-Attas, by whom she had three more sons and a daughter. Usama was raised in their modest white stucco home in Jeddah. He eventually inherited 2.27 percent of his father's company, a net worth which exceeded $25 million.

His mother remembers her first-born as "a shy kid, very nice, very considerate. He has always been helpful. I tried to instill in him the fear and love of God, the respect and love for his family, neighbors and teachers."[5] As a boy he enjoyed watching television; *Bonanza* was his favorite show. When he was 10, Usama was enrolled briefly in a boarding school north of Beirut, Lebanon. Ironically, it was run by the Quakers, a Christian group that emphasizes pacifism. We wonder how different history would have been if Usama had remained their student.

He returned home to Jeddah, where his mother enrolled him in the Al-Thaghr Model School, a very elite private high school. Like his fellow students, Usama wore Western clothing and learned English. Here he met a physical education teacher whose influence would change his life.

The man was a follower of the Muslim Brotherhood, a radical Islamist organization dedicated to the overthrow of Western influence in the Middle East. At the age of 15, Bin Laden was attracted to the gym teacher's after-school study group; he would later refer to his immersion in its ideology as his "conversion." He began fasting on Monday and Thursday in emulation of the Prophet Muhammad, and became increasingly impassioned by the plight of the Palestinians.

He was also engaged in his family's business by this time, receiving enough money to buy several luxury cars and pursue horseback riding, his favorite hobby. He went big-game hunting in Kenya and mountain climbing in Turkey. He enrolled in Jeddah's King Abdulaziz University in 1976 to study business administration. Muhammad Qutb, one of the intellectual leaders of radical Islam, was a lecturer at the university. Here bin Laden read *Milestones*, by Muhammad's brother Sayyid, one of the foundational documents of their militant movement. Among his teachers was Dr. Abdullah Azzam, a member of the Muslim Brotherhood and founder of Hamas (the radical movement that seeks to destroy Israel).

While in college, bin Laden married Najwa, a daughter of his mother's brother; he was 17, she was 14. She soon became pregnant and gave birth to a son, Abdullah, the first of their 11 children.

Though bin Laden later claimed to have graduated from university, independent accounts state that he left school a year short of graduation to work in his family's business. He secured an apartment in Jeddah, where he took a second wife in 1982. She held a Ph.D. in child psychology and taught at King Abdulaziz University; the couple had one child, a son. A few years later he married again, to a woman who held a doctorate in Arabic grammar and would bear him three daughters and a son. He would later take a fourth wife, who bore him three children as well.

As their family grew, bin Laden insisted that his children be raised in a very strict environment. Cartoons and television were banned (except for news programs); his children could not drink from straws, as they were unknown during the time of the Prophet. They made one trip to the West, seeking medical treatment for a son who suffered from hydrocephalus.

Bin Laden began working for the family company in Mecca, managing projects and using his ability with English to work with Western engineers. His income at this time was at least $150,000 a year.

Building "the Lion's Den"

By this time the Soviet invasion of Afghanistan was several years old. More and more Muslims were rallying to the Afghan cause, especially those who were motivated by militant ideology. Dr. Azzam, bin Laden's university teacher, had become a fundraiser for the Afghan resistance. He led his former student into the cause, turning his life from business to war and eventually to the Tuesday morning that changed our nation forever.

The Soviet oppression of Afghanistan represented everything about non-Muslims which bin Laden had come to hate. He interpreted their invasion as an attack on Islam itself and began rallying support for the Afghan resistance.

His primary weapon was financial. Bin Laden and Azzam established the *Maktab al-Khidmat*, the Services Bureau, which they used to set up a recruiting network for fighters and finances. Azzam ran the network, while bin Laden financed it by raising enormous funds for the war effort.

How was he able to secure such support? Giving to charity is one of the "five pillars" of Islam. Many wealthy families in Saudi Arabia arrange for their benevolence through a trusted third party that serves as their financial advisor. Given his contacts throughout Saudi society, bin Laden worked with many estates to channel funds to the fight for Islam in Afghanistan.

He not only waged "financial jihad"—he also provided personal hospitality for Arab recruits on their way to the front lines. Azzam then led bin Laden to join the war effort in Afghanistan personally. Here he came to the attention of a brilliant Egyptian eye surgeon who was a leader of the resistance: Ayman al-Zawahiri. The doctor, six years older than bin Laden, soon became a mentor to *him. He drew bin Laden into his circle and became his personal physician. Bin Laden had already contracted malaria and nearly died of pneumonia. By this time he had developed other physical ailments* that would plague him for the rest of his life: low blood pressure, weight loss, muscle fatigue, back pain, and intestinal discomfort. (Some physicians suggest that he may have suffered from Addison's disease, a diagnosis that would explain his symptoms.)

Bin Laden and Zawahiri built a small band of fighters loyal to their leadership. They built a base that they named "the Lion's Den" in honor of Usama. When he led them into battle in the spring of 1987, bin Laden stepped from business manager to battlefield hero. Towering over most of his soldiers (reports list his height as 6 feet 4 inches to 6 feet 6 inches), the willingness of this extremely wealthy tycoon to risk his life personally for the cause elevated his status to near myth among his followers. In gratitude for his military leadership, bin Laden was given a trophy from a dead Russian officer—the Kalikov AK-74 assault rifle with which he was so often pictured in the years afterward.

From freedom fighters to international terrorism

When the Soviets withdrew from Afghanistan in 1988, bin Laden consolidated his soldiers into a permanent militia. He and Zawahiri joined forces to lead their movement. On August 20, 1988, they and their followers established their formal organization, *Al Qaeda Al-Askariya* ("The Military Base"). They were 30 in number.

Using his strengths in fundraising, business management, and political connections, bin Laden began expanding his organization. He and Zawahiri built an impressive leadership council, including experts in military operations, weapons procurement, computers, media, tanks, mortars, and explosives. New recruits filled out forms in triplicate, swore themselves to secrecy, and pledged an oath of allegiance to bin Laden. Single members received $1,000 a month in salary; married members were paid $1,500. Every member received a month of vacation and a paid round-trip ticket home each year; there was a health care plan for the entire group. They constructed a constitution and by-laws, and became an attractive employer in a region where jobs were meager.

By 1989 bin Laden had received some $18 million from the family business (some place the number as high as $30 million), funds he dedicated to his organization. He returned to Saudi Arabia at the age of 31 as a war hero and began supporting Islamist rebels in South Yemen in their fight against their communist government.

Then came Saddam Hussein's invasion of Kuwait in 1990. From there he could advance on the Eastern Province of Saudi Arabia and seize control of the bulk of the world's oil supply. Bin Laden offered the support of his militia in expelling Saddam's advance, promising to marshal 100,000 volunteers in defense of his homeland.

At this time the Saudi army numbered only 58,000 men, facing an enemy with a standing army of nearly a million men. Bin Laden promised to defeat Iraq as his forces had defeated the Soviets, but his government turned instead to the hated "infidels" of the West, allowing Americans on sacred Saudi soil. Usama was outraged, and made his anger clear. He founded the Advice and Reform Committee, an organization with offices in Sudan and London that was devoted to anti-Saudi propaganda. He also continued his support for the rebels in Yemen, a movement that worried the Saudi government. On May 1, 1991, bin Laden left his native land as an exile.

He took his four wives and numerous children to Khartoum, Sudan. A 1989 coup there had installed a militant-Islamist regime whose ideology was attractive to bin Laden. He soon began channeling funds to his adopted base of operations; some reports place the figure as high as $350 million.

He set up an "Islamic Army Shura" to coordinate the terrorist groups with which he was building alliances. His organization began branching into multiple theaters of operations, sending money and materials to jihadist groups in Jordan, Eritrea, the Philippines, Pakistan, Egypt, Lebanon, Yemen, and Chechnya. These efforts cemented al-Qaeda as a keystone for international jihad.

Bin Laden lived in a luxury villa and worked out of an office in Khartoum's business district. During this time his family in Saudi Arabia made numerous attempts to persuade him to cease his militant activities and return home, but he rebuffed them all. His mother even made one such effort. In 1993, his family expelled him as a shareholder in their companies; in 1994 they repudiated him publicly.

During his years in Sudan, bin Laden expanded al-Qaeda from a group of combat fighters into an international terrorist organization. In 1996, under pressure from Saudi Arabia and the United States, the Sudanese government expelled him. Ironically, they offered to extradite him to the U.S. or Saudi Arabia, but both refused to take him. He moved his family again, this time returning to Afghanistan.

Declaring war on America

In 1996, bin Laden connected with Mullah Muhammad Omar, the leader of the Taliban, and moved his operations to Omar's base in Kandahar. As in Sudan, his financial support for Taliban leaders soon secured their support for his leadership. He provided them with great quantities of cash and imported Toyota Land Cruisers for their use. He funded hospitals and distributed food.

He soon published his first personal declaration of war against America and the West. It runs to 19 single-spaced pages in English. In his *fatwa* (a legal pronouncement issued by a religious leader) he stated of his followers, "They have no intention except to enter paradise by killing you.

An infidel, and enemy of God like you, cannot be in the same hell with his righteous executioner."[6]

The next year, bin Laden granted an interview to CNN's Peter Arnett. He branded America "the leader of terrorism and crime in the world," citing the bombing of Hiroshima and Nagasaki, and characterized his movement as "fulfilling a duty which God, Praise and Glory be to Him, decreed to us."[7]

During these years and moves, bin Laden continued to expand his al-Qaeda network. In 1998 he reunited with Zawahiri. The two issued a *fatwa* that laid the foundation for terrorism to come: "The ruling to kill the Americans and their allies—civilians and military—is an individual duty for every Muslim who can do it in any country in which it is possible to do it."[8] This decision to target civilians was apparently prompted by Zawahiri and rejects the protection of noncombatants that is consistent with more traditional Islam.

In May 1998, bin Laden granted another interview to an American journalist, this time speaking with ABC's John Miller. In explaining his intention to attack noncombatants, bin Laden claimed:

> The terrorism we practice is of the commendable kind for it is directed at the tyrants and the aggressors and the enemies of Allah, the tyrants, the traitors who commit acts of treason against their own countries and their own faith and their own prophet and their own nation. Terrorizing those and punishing them are necessary measures to straighten things and to make them right. Tyrants and oppressors who subject the Arab nation to aggression ought to be punished.[9]

As self-proclaimed leader of militant Islam, bin Laden had provided financial and rhetorical support for his movement. But his organization had not yet attacked its enemies directly. On August 7, 1998 (the eighth anniversary of the United States' landing in Saudi Arabia for Operation Desert Storm), two of his cells struck al-Qaeda's first blow against the United States. Suicide truck bombers attacked our embassies in Kenya and Tanzania, killing 224 and injuring more than 4,500. Bin Laden was eventually indicted by our federal government for his role in this crime, a charge that stood until his death.

By this time he had met Khalid Sheikh Muhammad, a Pakistani who had joined the militant cause. When Muhammed's nephew was arrested by U.S. forces, he conceived of a reply that would become known as the "planes operation." Muhammed initially wanted to hijack 10 planes and use them to attack American targets. Bin Laden felt the plan was too ambitious; the two eventually settled on a smaller strategy that bin Laden agreed to finance.

In attacking our embassies, bin Laden assaulted our political leadership. On October 12, 2000, he struck against our military when al-Qaeda suicide bombers attacked the USS. *Cole* in a Yemeni port, killing 17 Americans and wounding 39 others. The Clinton administration responded by mounting a cruise missile attack on Afghanistan which nearly killed bin Laden. Usama's motivation for the bombing was clear, and explains the strategy behind the 9/11 attacks that followed the next year: "We did the *Cole* and we wanted the United States to react. And if they reacted, they are going to invade Afghanistan and that's what we want . . . Then we will start holy war against the Americans, exactly like the Soviets."[10]

In 2001, bin Laden merged his organization formerly with Zawahiri's Egyptian Islamic Jihad, growing his movement to a core of 200 people, a 122-person martyrdom brigade and several dozen foot soldiers. Then came Khalid Sheikh Muhammad's strike against American targets on Tuesday morning, September 11, 2001. When the U.S. responded by invading Afghanistan and Iraq, bin Laden was delighted: "I am rejoicing in the fact that America has become embroiled in the quagmires of the Tigris and Euphrates. . . . Here is America today, screaming at the top of its voice as it falls apart in front of the whole world."[11]

Usama bin Laden had achieved his goal. His actions against the West provoked a military response that he could characterize as an attack on Islam itself. He was convinced that Muslims around the Arab world would rally to the defense of their faith under his leadership. They would expel American influence from their lands, topple governments loyal to the West, push Israel into the sea, and build a base for global Islamic expansion.

Exile and death

The results were not what he expected. Most of the Muslim world rejected his attacks on innocent Americans as unwarranted and viewed them as violations of the Qur'an. The United States' military engagements in Iraq and Afghanistan were successful in scattering bin Laden's organization and killing or capturing many of his key leaders.

Bin Laden was forced into hiding himself. Forced to communicate with the outer world through occasional videotapes, he maintained a stealth existence.

Meanwhile, terrorists captured after the 9/11 attacks identified one of bin Laden's most trusted couriers, a protégé of Khalid Sheikh Muhammed, the confessed mastermind of 9/11. Intelligence officers sought this courier for two years, then tracked him for two more. In August 2010 they discovered that he lived with his brother and their families in an unusual and extremely high-security building.

The three-story, fortress-like compound is eight times larger than nearby houses. It is located in Abbottabad, a summer resort 35 miles north of the Pakistani capital of Islamabad. The house stands a third of a mile from the Pakistan Military Academy. The town is headquarters for the Second Division of the Northern Army Corps; many officers retire there.

The compound is surrounded by 12- to 18-foot outer walls topped with barbed wire and contains two security gates. Few windows face the outside; the terrace has a seven-foot privacy wall. Residents burned their trash rather than putting it on the street for collection. The property is valued at $1 million but has no telephone or Internet service. Authorities determined that the residents had no explainable source of wealth and that it was far too secure to shield a mere courier. They concluded that the compound likely harbored bin Laden.

Authorities intended to capture the terrorist but assumed he would resist. They launched a helicopter raid on the compound early on Sunday morning, May 1, dropping members of an elite Navy SEALs team into the building. Bin Laden was hiding there with his youngest wife.

After 40 minutes of fighting, the SEALs found bin Laden and shot him in the head and chest. Three other adults were killed as well: two of his couriers and one of his adult sons. Two others were wounded. President Obama and senior government officials watched the operation in real-time in the White House Situation Room.

Bin Laden was identified through facial recognition techniques. One of his wives living with him in the compound identified him as well. CIA analysis found a "virtually 100 percent" match between his DNA and that of several members of his family.

His body was taken to Afghanistan after he was killed in Pakistan. Finding a country willing to accept the remains of the world's most wanted terrorist would have been difficult. His burial would also have created a shrine to him as a martyr in the mind of radical Islamists.

The body of Usama bin Laden was handled in accordance with traditional Islamic practice requiring burial within 24 hours. It was washed in accordance with Islamic custom, placed in a white sheet and then inside a weighted bag. A military officer aboard the aircraft carrier USS *Carl Vinson* in the North Arabian Sea read religious rites translated into Arabic. The body was then placed on a board and lowered into the sea.

Was bin Laden's death just?

I was working at home on the evening of May 1 when my wife called to tell me that the president was about to make an announcement of historic significance. I rushed to the television, where commentators were speculating as to the nature of the event. Word soon began leaking that Usama bin Laden had been killed. By the time President Obama made his formal announcement, much of the world had already heard the news.

The response in America was almost universal euphoria. He had been our "most wanted" criminal for a decade and was responsible for the deaths of thousands of Americans and war expenditures nearing a trillion dollars. If he had died in a bombing raid or while firing on American soldiers, few would have raised questions regarding the manner of his death. But he was unarmed when he was killed by Navy SEALs during a raid that our forces initiated on his compound. Was it right for our soldiers to take his life in this way?

Pragmatic factors soon became clear: the SEALs had no way to know if bin Laden was armed or even wired with explosives; they were in Pakistan without permission of that government and operating in a closing time window; if they had captured bin Laden, what kind of security nightmare would we face in imprisoning and trying him?

While these practical considerations may well justify the split-second decision by the SEALs to fire on bin Laden, the issue raises for many the larger question of "just war"—when is aggression against an enemy justified?

The 20th century was the bloodiest in human history. In World War I, 39 million people died (30 million were civilians); in World War II, 51 million died (including 34 million civilians); since World War II, approximately 150 wars have killed an estimated 16 million people worldwide. Were these wars just? How are we to measure?

"Total pacifism"

"Total pacifism" proponents argue that war is never justified under any circumstance. They might adopt non-violent means of opposing their enemies such as hunger strikes or public rallies, but they refuse to take up arms against others. Many cite Jesus' admonition: "Do not resist an evil person. If someone strikes you on the right cheek, turn to him the other also" (Matthew 5:39).

However, his words related to personal slander rather than self-defense or war. The left hand was never used in public in Jesus' culture; if I strike you on the right cheek with my right hand, I must slap you with the back of my hand. This is not a life-threatening attack but an insult. The context of Jesus' words clarifies their relational intent: "If someone wants to sue you and take your tunic, let him have your cloak as well. If someone forces you to go one mile, go with him two miles. Give to the one who asks you, and do not turn away from the one who wants to borrow from you" (vs. 40-42). His injunction was not intended to address the issue of just war.

Nonetheless, total pacifists believe that it is always wrong to injure or kill others, whatever their aggression toward us. They would obviously consider the killing of bin Laden to be immoral, whatever its circumstances.

"Initiatory war"

At the opposite end of the spectrum, "initiatory war" proponents argue that war is justified to protect ourselves from real or perceived threats. They assert that the technology of modern warfare makes it possible for an enemy to launch strikes such as 9/11 without warning, requiring us to anticipate such attacks and prevent them through any means necessary. For instance, while our declaration of war in response to Japan's December 7, 1941 attack on Pearl Harbor was easy to justify morally, many lives would have been spared if we had launched a preemptive attack against Japan's fleet on December 6.

Initiatory war supporters often claim justification for their position in God's command that his people initiate war against the Canaanites whose lands they had come to claim. He ordered them to destroy the inhabitants of Jericho (Joshua 6:5) and Ai (Joshua 8:1-2); after Joshua's death, he sent his people on continued attacks against various Canaanite peoples and cities (cf. Judges 1:1-4).

These people had done nothing to the Hebrews. They had not attacked them and were defending lands that had been theirs for centuries. But God knew that if they were left alive in the Promised Land, their paganism, idolatry and immorality would infect his people and lead to their rebellion against his word and will.

Moses warned the people about sins they would encounter among the Canaanites: "Let no one be found among you who sacrifices his son or daughter in the fire, who practices divination or sorcery, interprets omens, engages in witchcraft, or casts spells, or who is a medium or spiritist or who consults the dead" (Deuteronomy 18:10-11). The Canaanites were under his judgment precisely as a result of such sins: "because of these detestable practices the LORD your God will drive out those nations before you" (v. 12). So he led his chosen people to launch a preemptive attack against their Canaanite enemies. Those who advocate initiatory war find justification here for their position.

Of course, this logic is not compelling for everyone. First, the Hebrews were under direct mandate of the God who is "holy, holy, holy" (Isaiah 6:3); what human leader can claim such divine character and omniscience? Second, the conquest of Canaan was a one-time event necessary to create the nation through whom God would one day bring the Savior of the world, not a strategy prescribed for all people at all times. Third, if it is morally appropriate to initiate aggression against a nation or person merely because they have the capacity to harm us, what real or potential enemy are we not justified in attacking?

"Just war"

In the middle position, "just war" proponents believe that aggression against others can be justified under certain conditions. Cicero was the first to argue for such an approach,[12] but St. Augustine (AD 354-430) set forth its classic formulation:

- Just cause —a defensive war, fought only to resist aggression.
- Just intent—fought to secure justice, not for revenge, conquest, or money.
- Last resort—all other attempts to resolve the conflict have clearly failed.
- Legitimate authority—military force is authorized by the proper governmental powers.
- Limited goals—achievable, seeking a just peace.
- Proportionality—the good gained must justify the harm done.
- Noncombatant immunity—civilians protected as far as is humanly possible.

As you can see, the application of each criterion can be debated. Did we "resist aggression" by invading Afghanistan and Iraq to prevent further attacks by al-Qaeda? Did we defend Kuwait from Saddam Hussein in 1990 only to "secure justice," or were our oil interests a motivation? When have we reached "last resort," so that we can be certain that all other attempts to resolve the conflict have failed?

How are we to define the "proper governmental powers" for each nation? For instance, Saddam Hussein claimed that Iraq's constitution authorized him to invade Kuwait. Is armed aggression "limited" to military activity, or is nation-building sometimes needed to create a "just peace"? Who determines that the good gained has justified the harm—the winners or the losers? Must armed forces sometimes engage noncombatants in order to end the war, as with the bombings of Hiroshima and Nagasaki?

The killing of bin Laden

By these standards, was the killing of Usama bin Laden just? Pacifists would of course reject all armed aggression; those who support initiatory war would claim that bin Laden posed a mortal threat to our soldiers and nation. It seems to me that the action against bin Laden met each of the seven just war criteria: it responded to his aggression against America, seeking to secure justice after all other attempts to arrest him had failed; it was authorized by the president, advanced peace by removing al-Qaeda's most significant leader, led to a greater good for America and the West, and protected noncombatants as far as possible.

Whatever our position on bin Laden's death, Christians should view his passing with regret. Jesus taught us to "love your enemies and pray for those who persecute you" (Matthew 5:44). Our Lord's heart is clear: "I take no pleasure in the death of the wicked, but rather that they turn from their ways and live" (Ezekiel 33:11).

Do terrorists deserve the death penalty?

One other question regarding the life and death of Usama bin Laden remains to be addressed: Should his killing be viewed as a kind of capital punishment? How should we view the death penalty, especially with regard to terrorists?

"Capital punishment" derives its name from the Latin *caput*, meaning "head, top or leader." A "capital" crime is the most serious, a crime at the top of the list. Punishment for such a crime is thus "capital" as well.

Abolitionists and supporters debate three issues. One is *retribution*. Supporters argue that capital punishment is the equivalent and appropriate response to capital crimes, and that victims of a capital crime deserve justice. In their view, Usama bin Laden's death would be a justified consequence of his crimes and may bring some measure of closure to the survivors of 9/11. Abolitionists counter that enforcing the death penalty brutalizes society, and that life in prison is a worse punishment than death. They claim that killing people for killing people is illogical and teaches violence to society.

A second issue is *premeditation*. Supporters claim that capital punishment, if consistently applied, would have a deterrent effect on premeditated crime. Finding and killing bin Laden sends a signal to other terrorists that they cannot evade the consequences of their actions. Abolitionists argue that most murders are not premeditated and that evidence for deterrence is mixed at best. For example: in 2008 the average murder rate for states using capital punishment was 5.2 per 100,000 people; in states without a death penalty it was 3.3 per 100,000. However, another study indicates that each execution decreases homicides by about five.

A third argument relates to *protection of society*. Supporters state the obvious: a murderer who is executed cannot murder again. Usama bin Laden is no longer a danger to America. Abolitionists cite DNA evidence exonerating some convicts, including several who had been executed by the state. They point to the disproportionate number of minorities who are executed in the United States as evidence of discrimination. And they cite economic factors: Florida, for instance, spends $3.2 million per execution, six times the cost of life imprisonment.

Biblical arguments can be cited on both sides of the argument. In support of capital punishment:

- "For your lifeblood I will surely demand an accounting. I will demand an accounting from every animal. And from each man, too, I will demand an accounting for the life of his fellow man. 'Whoever sheds the blood of man, by man shall his blood be shed; for in the image of God has God made man'" (Genesis 9:5-6).
- "If anyone takes the life of a human being, he must be put to death. Anyone who takes the life of someone's animal must make restitution—life for life" (Leviticus 24:17-18).
- "Stone him to death, because he tried to turn you away from the LORD your God, who brought you out of Egypt, out of the land of slavery. Then all Israel will hear and be afraid, and no one among you will do such an evil thing again" (Deuteronomy 13:10-11).

Theologians who argue against capital punishment counter that the Genesis statement is descriptive of that early period in human history, not prescriptive for all time. They note that the Leviticus and Deuteronomy injunctions are not repeated in the New Testament, a key test in determining whether Old Testament laws retain prescriptive force today. And they point out that God did not seek the death of Cain, Moses or David for their capital crimes.

Both sides can cite Paul's assertion:

Everyone must submit himself to the governing authorities, for there is no authority except that which God has established. The authorities that exist have been established by God. Consequently, he who rebels against the authority is rebelling against what God has instituted, and those who do so will bring judgment on themselves. For rulers hold no terror for those who do right, but for those who do wrong. Do you want to be free from fear of the one in authority? Then do what is right and he will commend you. For he is God's servant to do you good. But if you do wrong, be afraid, for he does not bear the sword for nothing. He is God's servant, an agent of wrath to bring punishment on the wrongdoer. Therefore, it is necessary to submit to the authorities, not only because of possible punishment but also because of conscience (Romans 13:1-5).

Proponents point to the "sword" wielded by the state as endorsement of capital punishment for criminals like bin Laden; opponents relate the reference to punishment, not execution.

Conclusion

Usama bin Laden was an obscure member of a prominent Saudi family who became the global face of terrorism. His story is not yet done. Consider the insight of Khaled Abou El Fadl, a recognized Islamic scholar and professor at the UCLA School of Law. He warns that Usama bin Laden is "representative of underlying currents in contemporary Islam" and calls his followers "the children of a profound dissonance and dysfunctionalism."[13]

As we will see, bin Laden's "children" are the greatest threat our children have ever faced.

ENDNOTES

1.   Arabic can be difficult to transliterate into English. While bin Laden's first name is usually spelled "Osama" in English, "Usama" is closer to the original Arabic and is the spelling followed in most government documents.

2.   http://www.fbi.gov/wanted/topten, accessed 17 June 2011.

3.   Sources consulted for this chapter include: Jed Babbin, *In the Words of Our Enemies* (Washington, D.C.: Regnery Publishing, 2007); Daniel Benjamin and Steven Simon, *The Age of Sacred Terror: Radical Islam's War with America* (New York: Random House, 2003); John L. Esposito, *Unholy War: Terror in the Name of Islam* (New York: Oxford University Press, 2002); Efraim Karsh, *Islamic Imperalism: A History*, updated edition (New Haven, Connecticut: Yale University Press, 2007); Bernard Lewis, *The Crisis of Islam: Holy War and Unholy Terror* (New York: Random House, 2003); *The 9/11 Commission Report*, authorized edition (New York: W.W. Horton, n.d.); and Lawrence Wright, *The Looming Tower: Al-Qaeda and the Road to 9-11* (New York: Vintage Books, 2006). This chapter is especially indebted to Steve Coll's authoritative study of the bin Laden family: *The Bin Ladens: An Arabian Family in the American Century* (New York: The Penguin Press, 2008).

4.   "Mohamed" is the most frequent English spelling of bin Laden's first name. For purposes of consistency, I will spell all other occurrences of the name as "Muhammad," the most common English transliteration of the Arabic.

5.   Quoted in Coll, 158.

6.   Quoted in Babbin, 9.

7.   Ibid., 13.

8.   Ibid., 13.

9.   Ibid., 16.

10. Quoted in Coll 511.

11. Ibid., 568.

12. http://www.allsaintscville.org/Week%203-%20Just%20War%20%28Augustine%29.pdf

13. Khaled Abou El Fadl, *The Great Theft: Wrestling Islam From the Extremists* (New York: HarperOne, 2007) 101.

CHAPTER TWO

WHAT DO MUSLIMS BELIEVE? WHAT DISTINGUISHES RADICAL AND ORTHODOX MUSLIMS?

I am alive today because of a Muslim I have never met.

During the summer of 1979, I lived in East Malaysia, on the western coast of the island of Borneo in Southeast Asia. My job was to visit jungle villages and coastal cities, working as a missionary on behalf of Baptist churches. Because the dense rainforest made roads from town to town virtually impassable, transportation was via Malaysia Air Services, or MAS for short. The locals explained that the letters stood for "May Arrive Sometime." One time, we nearly didn't.

In those days MAS flew twin-prop airplanes functioning as buses for the masses. On various occasions I sat next to a goat, a chicken in a coop, and a mother with three small children in her lap. Nearly all our very brief flights were uneventful. Then came the day we tried to land in a thunderstorm. Our ancient aircraft bucked and strained in the gale-force winds. Lightning flashed outside our windows. Roiling clouds hid the jungles beneath us. Even the seasoned travelers around me winced in fear.

Suddenly the clouds broke and the ground rushed up at us. Our pilot gracefully glided our airplane to the runway with a gentle thud. When his grateful passengers began to deplane, he stood beside the door and thanked each one for flying with his airline. As I passed by him, I noted the prayer callus on his forehead and knew that he was a zealous Muslim, bowing his head frequently to his prayer rug as he prayed five times each day.

Since that day, I have met and befriended Muslims the world over. From Australia to Turkey, from Bangladesh to Egypt and Israel, from São Paulo to Dallas, I have been privileged to know Muslims on six continents. With one exception (a story I'll tell in chapter 9), every encounter has been a privilege. While I have taught world religions for more than 25 years, I have learned more about Islam from its followers than from all the text-books I have studied.

Islam can mean "peace," "submission," or "surrender." "Muslims" are followers of Islam. (*Muslim* is the participle of the verb for which "Islam" is the infinitive.) Islam is the religion of more than 1.6 billion people on our planet.

What do they believe? What convictions distinguish radical Muslims from the rest of Islam? Let's explore briefly the "Five Pillars of Islam," then discover the two tenets that separate radical and orthodox Muslims.[1]

Shahadah (the Creed)

The first pillar of Islam is its creed, the shortest of any major world religion: *La ilaha illa Allah, Muhammad rasul Allah* ("There is no God but God, and Muhammad is his prophet"). This statement, always recited in Arabic, is the Islamic profession of faith. By analogy, Jews recite the *Shema*: "Hear, O Israel: The Lord our God, the Lord is one" (Deuteronomy

6:4), and Christians state as their profession of faith, "Jesus is Lord": "If you confess with your mouth, 'Jesus is Lord,' and believe in your heart that God raised him from the dead, you will be saved" (Romans 10:9). In the same way, Muslims recite the *Shahadah* as their foundational faith statement.

Their creed is taken directly from the Qur'an, their holy book: "Your God is One God: there is no God but He, Most Gracious, Most Merciful" (2:163); "Obey God and His Apostle" (3:32).[2] The *Shahadah* are the first words Muslims hear when they are born and the last they hope to hear when they die. The creed is repeated five times each day as Muslims say their prayers. A person who states the *Shahadah* as his or her personal conviction, in the presence of two witnesses, becomes a convert to Islam. As we will see, winning the world to Islam and the *Shahadah* is the ultimate goal of radical Muslims.

Salat (Prayers)

My first morning in East Malaysia, I was awakened at dawn by a sound I had never heard before—the Muslim call to prayer. From the minaret of a nearby mosque came the chant heard in Muslim countries five times each day:

> *Allahu Akbar* (God is great!), repeated four times.
> *Ashhadu an la ilaha ilallah* (I bear witness that there is no god but God), repeated twice.
> *Ashhadu anna auhammadar rasulullah* (I bear witness that Muhammad is Allah's messenger), repeated twice.
> *Hayya 'alal salah* (Rush to prayer), repeated twice.
> *Hayya 'alal falah* (Rush to success), repeated twice.
> *Allahu Akbar* (God is great!), repeated twice.
> *La ilaha illal lah* (There is no god but God).

The five calls to prayer are known by their names and times: *Sobh* (dawn), *Dhuhr* (just after noon), *'Asr* (late afternoon), *Maghrib* (just after sunset), and *'Isha* (at night before retiring). The call to *Sobh* is issued the moment there is enough daylight to distinguish light and dark threads; *Maghrib* is issued when it is too dark to do the same. The first call to prayer is accompanied with the promise, *Assalatu khairum minan naum* ("Prayer is better than sleep").

These prayers are mandated by the Qur'an: "Verily, I am God: there is no god but I: so serve thou Me (only), and establish regular prayer for celebrating My praise" (20:14); "Set up regular Prayers: for such Prayers are enjoined on Believers at stated times" (4:103). Many Muslims believe that they will suffer great punishment from Allah if they miss their daily prayers.

Prayers are typically offered on a small rug while facing the *Ka'ba* in Mecca (to be explained in chapter 3). Muslims first wash themselves, as "God loves those who turn to him constantly and He loves those who keep themselves pure and clean" (2:222). Their washing rituals are set out clearly:

> O ye who believe! when ye prepare for prayer, wash your faces, and your hands (and arms) to the elbows; rub your heads (with water); and (wash) your feet to the ankles. If ye are in a state of ceremonial impurity, bathe your whole body. But if ye are ill, or on a journey, or one of you cometh from offices of nature, or ye have been in contact with women, and ye find no water, then take for yourselves clean sands or earth, and rub therewith your faces and hands. God doth not wish to place you in a difficulty, but to make you clean, and to complete his favour to you, that ye may be grateful (5:6).

Properly prepared, Muslims then perform the *rak'ah*—they stand, then bow to the ground twice, touching their foreheads to the ground.

(I have known many Muslims whose forehead calluses bear testimony to their lifelong obedience in prayer.) They utter *Allahu Akbar* (God is great), then recite verses from the Qur'an. They do this 17 times, touching their foreheads to the ground 34 times, speaking their obligatory prayers in Arabic whether they understand the language or not. They can then pray in their own language if they wish.

Their central prayer, functioning like The Lord's Prayer for Christians, is the first chapter of the Qur'an:

> *In the name of God, Most Gracious, most Merciful.*
> *Praise be to God, the Cherisher and Sustainer of the Worlds;*
> *Most Gracious, Most Merciful;*
> *Master of the Day of Judgement.*
> *Thee do we worship and Thine aid we seek.*
> *Show us the straight way.*
> *The way of those on whom Thou hast bestowed thy Grace, those whose*
> *(portion) is not wrath, and who go not astray (1:1-7)*

On Friday, the holy day in Islam, Muslims pray just after noon in the "mosque" (*masjid*, "the place of prostration"). Muhammad built the first mosque in April, A.D. 623. It was a rough building with a roof supported by tree trunks. All future mosques would follow its simple model as much as possible.

A stone known as the *qiblah* marks the direction of prayer toward Mecca. Men form lines to pray and to hear the sermon issued from the *Minbar* (pulpit) by a political or religious leader. There is no music or other form of worship in the service. Women and children pray in a separate room or from the balcony.

These Friday services are instrumental for disseminating political messages throughout the community. As we will see, this fact is important in understanding the growth of radical Islam.

Sawm (Fasting)

Ramadan is the ninth month of the Muslim lunar calendar. (It comes 10 days earlier each year on our solar calendars.) Muslims believe that Muhammad received his first revelation on the 17th day of this month, making it the holiest month of the year: "Ramadhan [sic] is the (month) in which was sent down the Qur'an, as a guide to mankind, also clear (Signs) for guidance and judgement (between right and wrong)" (2:185).

As a result, they set aside the month for consecration. The Qur'an has been divided into 30 equal parts so it can be read in its entirety during Ramadan. Central to Muslim devotion is the discipline of fasting: "O ye who believe! Fasting is prescribed to you as it was prescribed to those before you, that ye may (learn) self restraint,—(Fasting) for a fixed number of days" (2:183-184). This discipline is linked to Ramadan: "every one of you who is present (at his home) during that month should spend it in fasting" (2:185).

During Ramadan, Muslims swallow nothing from the first prayer of the day to the fourth. They also refrain from smoking and sexual relations during the day. During the evening they can eat and feast as they wish. They pray more fervently during this month and especially on *Lailatul Qadr* (the "Night of Power"), the night when Muhammad received his first revelation:

> We have indeed revealed this (Message) in the Night of Power; And what will explain to thee what the Night of Power is? The Night of Power is better than a thousand Months. Therein come down the angels and the Spirit by God's permission, on every errand: Peace! . . . This until the rise of Morn! (97:1-5).

Hajj (Pilgrimage)

Two million to three million Muslims make the *hajj* each year, traveling to Mecca in the 12th month of the Muslim year. They wear white robes while walking around the *Ka'ba*, a structure believed to have been constructed by Adam and rebuilt by Abraham and Ishmael. It contains a black stone that Muslims believe descended from heaven to mark the center of the world (see chapter 3).

The Qur'an calls Muslims to this pilgrimage: "Remember We made the House a place of assembly for men and a place of safety; and take ye the Station of Abraham as a place of prayer; and We covenanted with Abraham and Isma'il, that they should sanctify My House for those who compass it round, or use it as a retreat, or bow, or prostrate themselves (therein in Prayer)" (2:125). Muhammad performed this pilgrimage in A.D. 629 and required it of his followers.

Pilgrims cleanse themselves while outside Mecca, then walk counterclockwise around the *Ka'ba* seven times (the *tawaf*) while chanting *Labbayka Allahumma Labbayk* ("Here I am at your service, O God, here I am!").

Next they run seven times between two small hills (the *Sa'i*), reenacting Hagar's plight (cf. Genesis 16). They spend the night in the town of Mina, then journey to the plain of Arafat, where Muhammad preached his last sermon. Here they stand from afternoon to evening in honor of this event. They return to Mina, where they believe Abraham offered Ishmael (37:100-111). Note that Muslims reject the biblical record in Genesis 22 that Abraham sacrificed Isaac atop Mount Moriah. As we will see, this fact is very important in understanding radical Muslims' view of Israel.

Pilgrims then journey back to Mecca, where they walk around the *Ka'ba* seven more times. They run between the two hills again, return to Mina, then return a third time to Mecca for one more *tawaf*. Those who complete this pilgrimage are known as *Hajji* ("one who finished the hajj"). All Muslims are expected to make the *hajj* at least once in their lives. If they are physically unable to perform the pilgrimage, they are to pay the expenses for someone to go in their place.

Zakat (Alms)

The fifth Muslim pillar is obligatory almsgiving known as the *zakat*. The amount varies between 2.5 and 20 percent, depending on the goods taxed, whether agricultural, mineral, or livestock. The Qur'an specifies categories of people eligible to receive these alms: "Alms are for the poor and the needy, and those employed to administer the (funds); for those whose hearts have been (recently) reconciled (to Truth); for those in bondage and in debt; in the cause of God; and for the wayfarer; (thus is it) ordained by God, and God is full of knowledge and wisdom" (9:60).

Some countries such as Saudi Arabia, Malaysia, and Pakistan collect the *zakat* from their citizens. Others such as Lebanon, Bangladesh, Kuwait, and Bahrain regulate the *zakat*, but contributions are voluntary. In others, *zakat* committees collect the funds and distribute them.

To summarize, these five pillars summarize Muslim theology and practice:

- The creed: "There is no God but God, and Muhammad is his prophet."
- Prayers made five times each day while facing Mecca.
- Fasting during the holy month of Ramadan.
- Pilgrimage to Mecca at least once in a person's lifetime.
- Alms-giving to the poor.

Adherence to these requirements is essential to earning one's place in heaven.

Shari'a ("path")

Why do Muslims adhere to these five pillars? How do they practice them in their daily lives?

Shari'a is the code of conduct in Islam. To live by *Shari'a* is to practice the five pillars and all they entail. This code is derived from four sources: the Qur'an, Islam's holy book; the *Hadith*, a commentary on the Qur'an that transmits other sayings and actions of Muhammad; the *ijma*, a consensus of Muslim scholars on particular issues; and the *qiyas*, legal deductions based on these authoritative sources.

The foundation of Islam is the Qur'an ("recitation"), so named because of the angel Gabriel's command that Muhammad "recite" when he first received these revelations. (We'll learn its history in chapter 3.) The Qur'an repeatedly proclaims its divine origin:

- ◆ "It is He Who sent down to thee (step by step) in truth, the Book, confirming what went before it" (3:3).
- ◆ "And this is a Book which We have revealed as a blessing: so follow it and be righteous, that ye may receive mercy" (6:155).
- ◆ "For we had certainly sent unto them a Book, based on knowledge, which We explained in detail,—a guide and a mercy to all who believe" (7:52).
- ◆ "We have sent down to thee a Book explaining all things, a Guide, a mercy, and Glad Tidings to Muslims" (16:89).

The Qur'an is approximately the same length as the New Testament and is divided into 114 *suras* (chapters) containing approximately 6,200 verses, 80,000 words and 330,000 letters. Its chapters are arranged from longest to shortest rather than in a chronological fashion.

Muslims believe that God gave every word of the Qur'an directly to Muhammad through the angel Gabriel; he then repeated these exact words to listeners, who memorized and transcribed them. Since the Qur'an describes Muhammad as "the unlettered Prophet" (7:158), many Muslims believe that their Prophet was illiterate, making his role in this process even more miraculous.

The Qur'an is the most venerated object in Islam. In many Muslim societies, readers kiss the book three times before opening it to read, then kiss it three times and touch it to their foreheads after closing it. It is never left open and unattended and is always placed on the highest bookshelf in the home. The Qur'an is packed last in a suitcase and never carried below the waistline. It is never to touch the ground; when readers study the Qur'an while sitting on the ground they use special book holders made for this purpose.

Muslims usually refer to their holy book as the "Glorious Qur'an" or the "Noble Qur'an." They speak of it as *Kalimat Allah* ("the Word of God"), *al-Furqan* ("the Distinguisher"), or simply *al-Kitab* ("the Book").[3] The Qur'an is the final revelation of God for Muslims and the central focus of their faith and lives. All of life must be submitted to its revelation and laws.

In addition to the Qur'an, the *Hadith* ("reported speech") are a vital source of Islamic law. They collect what Muhammad said (*qawl*), what he did (*fi'l*), and what he approved (*taqrir*). These sayings, actions, and teachings were passed on verbally and then collected and transcribed. Sunni Muslims view six early collections, the "six major *Hadith*," as most important. Shiites include in the *Hadith* the sayings and deeds of the 12 Imams whom they believe were chosen to lead the Muslim community (see chapter 7).

The *Hadith* give us the *Sunnah* ("form" or "customary practice") of Muhammad, acts that others should seek to emulate:

- "If ye do love God, follow me" (3:31).
- "Obey God and His Apostle" (3:32).

- "Verily, this is My Way, leading straight: follow it: follow not (other) paths: they will scatter you about from His (great) Path: thus doth He command you, that ye may be righteous" (6:153).
- "Ye have indeed in the Apostle of God a beautiful pattern (of conduct) for any one whose hope is in God and the Final Day, and who engages much in the praise of God" (33:21).

The *ijma* ("consensus") of Muslim scholars on an issue constitutes a third source of Islamic authority. Sunnis place greater trust in the *ijma* than Shiites. The fourth source of authority are the *qiyas*, legal deductions based on the Qur'an and *Hadith*.

Shari'a developed over several centuries after Muhammad's death in A.D. 632. There is no single *Shari'a* code accepted by all Muslims. Rather, there are several "schools" of *Shari'a*, each named for the scholars who inspired them:

- Hanbali: the most fundamental; embraced in Saudi Arabia and by the Taliban.
- Hanafi: the most liberal, focused on reason and analogy; dominant in Central Asia, Egypt, Pakistan, India, China, Turkey.
- Malaki: dominant in North Africa.
- Shafi'i: followed in Indonesia, Malaysia, Brunei, Yemen.
- Ja'fari: Shi'a law.

Shari'a typically recognizes three categories of offenses: Those with punishments prescribed in the Qur'an, those that fall under a judge's discretion, and those resolved through tit-for-tat, such as blood money paid to the family of a murder victim. Qur'anic punishments (*hadd*) are required for unlawful sexual intercourse, false accusation of unlawful sexual intercourse, wine or alcohol drinking, theft, and highway robbery. Punishments include flogging, stoning, amputation, exile, and execution. They are not often carried out, though vigilante justice such as honor killings can be a major problem.

Shari'a can be related to the modern world in three ways. One is a dual legal system where the government is secular but Muslims can choose to bring familial and financial disputes to *Shari'a* courts. For instance, Britain now allows *Shari'a* tribunals governing marriage, divorce, and inheritance; this arrangement is similar to Anglican and Jewish mediation. Criminal law matters remain under the existing legal system.

At the other extreme is "government under God," where Islam is the official religion and *Shari'a* is the source of laws. This model is followed in Saudi Arabia, Kuwait, Bahrain, Yemen, and the United Arab Emirates. In Egypt, Pakistan, Iran, and Iraq, it is illegal to enact legislation that contradicts Islam. In Saudi Arabia, women are not allowed to drive, are under the guardianship of male relatives at all times, and must be completely covered in public.

A third option is a completely secular Muslim nation such as modern-day Turkey. Here Muslim dress is banned in universities and public buildings, and the government operates as a secular democracy, though movement toward an Islamic state is growing, as we will see in chapter 7.

Shari'a also affects financial systems. *Riba*, charging or paying interest, is banned under Islamic law. Transactions related to weapons, alcohol, tobacco, gambling, pornography, and pork are also banned. Banks such as Citigroup, HSBC, and Deutsche Bank are now developing Islamic banking sectors. By some estimates, Islamic banking is growing 15 percent a year. As we will see, the interpretation and application of *Shari'a* is directly related to the goals of radical Muslims.

Usama bin Laden explains 9/11

All Muslims affirm and seek to fulfill their five pillars. In addition to these tenets, two other convictions mark those who embrace a radical or militant form of Islam.

The best-known spokesperson for radical Islam was, of course, Usama bin Laden. On Sunday, November 24, 2002, he published a "Letter to America" in which he answered directly the question, "Why are we fighting and opposing you?"[4] Here we find a clear delineation of the two tenets of radical Islam.

The first tenet is expressed in bin Laden's first reply: "The answer is very simple: Because you attacked us and continue to attack us." Bin Laden claimed that America attacked the Muslim world in Palestine, Somalia, Chechnya, and Kashmir. He charged us with supporting governments in the Muslim world that "prevent our people from establishing the Islamic Shariah, using violence and lies to do so." Referring to OPEC's export of oil to the West, bin Laden alleged that "these governments steal our Ummah's wealth and sell them to you at a paltry price."

In other words, the first justification for 9/11 and other terrorism against the West is that we attacked Islam first. As we will see in the next chapter, this assertion is anchored in the Qur'anic requirement that Muslims defend Islam. It leads radical Muslims to believe that they are defending Islam by attacking us.

The second tenet of radical Islam is expressed in bin Laden's second explanation for 9/11: "You may then dispute that all the above [aggression against Islam] does not justify aggression against civilians, for crimes they did not commit and offenses in which they did not partake." His response is so important that I have quoted it in full:

> This argument contradicts your continuous repetition
> that America is the land of freedom, and its leaders in this
> world. Therefore, the American people are the ones who

choose their government by way of their own free will; a choice which stems from their agreement to its policies. Thus the American people have chosen, consented to, and affirmed their support for the Israeli oppression of the Palestinians, the occupation and usurpation of their land, and its continuous killing, torture, punishment and expulsion of the Palestinians. The American people have the ability and choice to refuse the policies of their Government and even to change it if they want.

The American people are the ones who pay the taxes which fund the planes that bomb us in Afghanistan, the tanks that strike and destroy our homes in Palestine, the armies which occupy our lands in the Arabian Gulf, and the fleets which ensure the blockade of Iraq. These tax dollars are given to Israel for it to continue to attack us and penetrate our lands. So the American people are the ones who fund the attacks against us, and they are the ones who oversee the expenditure of these monies in the way they wish, through their elected candidates.

Also the American army is part of the American people. It is this very same people who are shamelessly helping the Jews fight against us.

The American people are the ones who employ both their men and their women in the American Forces which attack us.

This is why the American people cannot be not innocent of all the crimes committed by the Americans and Jews against us.

Allah, the Almighty, legislated the permission and the option to take revenge. Thus, if we are attacked, then we have the right to attack back. Whoever has destroyed

our villages and towns, then we have the right to destroy
their villages and towns. Whoever has stolen our wealth,
then we have the right to destroy their economy. And
whoever has killed our civilians, then we have the right
to kill theirs.

To summarize bin Laden's logic: 9/11 was a justified attack against
the perpetrators of aggression against Islam. In his mind there are no
innocent Americans. Since we elect our leaders and support our government and military, we are each complicit in this perceived attack on the
Muslim world.

Viewed in this way, the Muslims who hijacked American jetliners
on September 11, 2001, were not mounting an unprovoked attack on
innocent citizens. Rather, their actions constituted a defense of Islam
that struck at the heart of Western, "crusader" imperialism. The Twin
Towers symbolized our financial oppression of Muslims; the Pentagon
represented our military attacks against the Muslim world; and the
White House (the apparent target of the fourth hijacking) signified our
political aggression against Islam.

The tenets of radical Islam

These two claims separate radical Muslims from orthodox followers
of Islam: (1) Muslims must take up arms to protect Islam from Western
aggression; and (2) all citizens of the Western world are enemies of Islam.
For militant Muslims, killing Americans by any means necessary is a
defense of Islam mandated by the Qur'an.

Consider some examples of the first tenet. Al-Qaeda spokesman
Suleiman Abu Gheith, defending 9/11: "What happened to America is
something natural, an expected event for a country that uses terror, arrogant policy, and suppression against the nations and the peoples, and

imposes a single method, thought, and way of life, as if the people of the entire world are clerks in its government offices and employed by its commercial companies and institutions."[5]

Gheith is convinced that "America is the reason for all oppression, injustice, licentiousness, or suppression that is the Muslims' lot. It stands behind all the disasters that were caused and are still being caused to the Muslims; it is immersed in the blood of Muslims and cannot hide this."[6]

Iran's Supreme Leader Ayatollah Ali Khamenei, speaking to pilgrims at the *hajj* on January 26, 2005, agreed:

> At present, the Islamic world is faced with an all-out siege, both on the economic and the technological fronts, as well as with a propaganda offensive, and most recently with military occupation. The occupation of Palestine and the holy city of Quds [Jerusalem] have culminated in the occupation of Iraq and Afghanistan. The Zionist octopus—along with the vicious and despicable U.S. imperialism—now harbors plans for the entire region of the Middle East, as well as North Africa and the entire Islamic world. . . .
>
> Imperialist arrogance has deployed all its capabilities to this end. It has launched this fateful war, using political pressure on one front, threats of economic sanctions on another, and employing propaganda tactics in one place and bombs, missiles, tanks, and troops in other places, such as Iraq and Afghanistan, just as it did before in Palestine and Quds. . . . They manufacture, supply, and use nuclear, chemical, and biological weapons of mass destruction. . . .
>
> They themselves are behind the dirty drug-trade mafia, but claim to be fighting the narcotics trade. They make a display of supporting science and the globalization

of science, and yet obstruct the development of science and technology in the Islamic world, considering the emergence of nuclear technology for peaceful purposes in Islamic countries a mortal sin.[7]

Khamenei claimed that militant Muslims defend Islam rather than initiating war with the West:

> We are not the kind of people to sit and wait for somebody to strike at us, without striking back. We are people of peace and tranquility. We do not attack anybody. The reason is obvious. What country did we ever attack? Against what country did we ever start a war? What country did we ever threaten? We are not the kind of people who do such things. But we are the kind of people that when attacked by anybody, we strike back twice as hard.[8]

The second tenet of radical Islam asserts that citizens in the West are the enemies of Islam since we elect our leaders and support our military. Sheikh Abdel Rahman, who planned the 1993 World Trade Center bombing, expressed this assertion clearly: "Oh, you Muslims everywhere, sever the ties of their nation, tear them apart, ruin their economy, instigate against their corporations, destroy their embassies, attack their interests, sink their ships, and shoot down their airplanes. Kill them in land, at sea, and in the air; kill them wherever you find them."[9]

Al-Qaeda spokesman Gheith issued a similar call to Muslims worldwide: "Wherever you are, kill those Jews and those Americans who are like them—and those who stand by them—they are all in one trench, against the Arabs and the Muslims."[10]

Saudi cleric Aed al-Qarni agreed: "I pray to Allah that He will make the enemies fall into their own trap and that He will destroy the Jews and their helpers from among the Christians and the Communists, and that He will turn them into the Muslims' spoils. . . . Houses and young men must be sacrificed. Throats must be slit and skulls must be shattered. This is the path to victory, to shahada [the Muslim creed], and to sacrifice.[11]

Iranian Secretary of the Guardian Council Ayatollah Ahmad Jannati joined this call against citizens of the West: "Every Muslim and every honorable man who is not a Muslim must stand against the Americans, English, and Israelis and endanger their interests wherever they may be. They must not have security. If Muslims have no security neither must they."[12]

Brigadier S. K. Malik's *The Quranic Concept of War* is an authoritative definition of *jihad* for militant Muslims. His statement is clear and chilling:

> The Quranic military strategy thus enjoins us to prepare ourselves for war to the utmost in order to strike terror into the hearts of our enemies, known or hidden, while guarding ourselves from being terror-stricken by the enemy. In this strategy, guarding ourselves against terror is the "Base," preparation for war to the utmost is the "Cause:" while striking terror into the hearts against the enemies is the "Effect." The whole philosophy revolves there. . . . In war, our main object is the opponent's heart or soul.[13]

Conclusion

Do all Muslims agree with the tenets of radical Islam? Abraham Sarker, a Muslim missionary to America before his conversion to Christianity, addressed our question:

> Islam's history and Holy Scripture clearly supply support for violent aggression against non-Muslims in order to establish Allah's right way on the earth. Several groups

of modern radical Muslims attest to this practice today. Most modern Muslims, however, believe that the season of fierce, hostile invasion of other lands and peoples pertained only to the initial spread of Islam, and should not be practiced today. They believe that Islam should spread through peaceful methods. According to this group, the only appropriate occasion for violent jihad is the necessary defense of Islam against assailants."[14]

In my travels throughout the Muslim world I have met followers of Islam who are among the most hospitable and peace-loving people I have ever known. I have also encountered Muslims in America and abroad who are convinced that aggression against the West is the duty of all Muslims.

Which posture is the true face of Islam? For guidance, we'll ask its founding Prophet.

ENDNOTES

1. Sources for this chapter include Kerby Anderson, *A Biblical Point of View on Islam* (Eugene, Oregon: Harvest House Publishers, 2007); Karen Armstrong, *Islam: A Short History* (New York: The Modern Library, 2002); Jed Babbin, *In the Words of Our Enemies* (Washington, D.C.: Regnery Publications, Inc., 2007); Mateen Elass, *Understanding the Koran: A Quick Christian Guide to the Muslim Holy Book* (Grand Rapids, Michigan: Zondervan, 2004); Mark A. Gabriel, *Jesus and Muhammad: Profound Differences and Surprising Similarities* (Lake Mary, Florida: Charisma House, 2004); Laurent Murawiec, *The Mind of Jihad* (New York: Cambridge University Press, 2008); Anis A. Shorrosh, *Islam Revealed: A Christian Arab's View of Islam* (Nashville, Tennessee: Thomas Nelson, 1988); and especially Abraham Sarker, *Understand My Muslim People* (Newberg, Oregon: Barclay Press, 2004). Dr. Sarker's book is the best introduction to Islam I have found and was instrumental to this study.

2. This study utilizes *The Qur'an: Text, Translation and Commentary*, by Abdullah Yusuf Ali (Elmhurst, New York: Tahrike Tarsile Qur'an, Inc.) U.S. edition 2005. Note that words in parentheses are supplied by the translator to clarify the meaning of the text.

3. Elass 8-14.

4. http://www.guardian.co.uk/world/2002/nov/24/theobserver, accessed 3 July 2011.

5. http://www.jewishpost.com/archives/news/why-we-fight-america-al-qaida-spokesman-explains-september-11-and-declares-intentions-to-kill-4-million-americans-with-weapons-of-mass-destruction.html, accessed 3 July 2011.

6. Ibid.

7. http://www.mail-archive.com/osint@yahoogroups.com/msg03535.html, accessed 4 July 2011.

8. Khamenei's Friday Sermon, April 26, 2006, quoted in Babbin 103-4.

9. http://query.nytimes.com/gst/fullpage.html?res=9B05E5DE153BF93BA35753C1A9629C8B63, accessed 4 July 2011.

10. Gheith, ibid.

11. http://www.terrorism-info.org.il/malam_multimedia/html/final/eng/memri/apr_c_05.htm, accessed 4 July 2011.

12. Quoted in Babbin 109-10.

13. Quoted in Murawiec, 322.

14. Sarker 199-200.

CHAPTER THREE

WHO WAS MUHAMMAD? WAS HE THE FIRST RADICAL MUSLIM?

Did Muhammad intend Islam to be a religion of tolerance, or was he the original radical Muslim?

Karen Armstrong, the famous historian of world religions, states categorically that "Muhammad was not a man of violence."[1] Wafa Sultan, a Syrian-born Muslim who later emigrated to the United States, states just as categorically, "Anyone who browses through the pages of Muslim history from the day Muhammad first declared his new religion until the present day will see at once how bloody it has been."[2]

Which view is more correct? Would the founder of Islam have affirmed the two tenets of its radical followers? What does his story say to our conflict with militant Muslims today?[3]

The businessman who changed history[4]

The Muslim world, defined as societies with Muslim majorities and/ or Muslim rulers, occupies more geography than Europe and the United States combined.[5] But before Islam was a global phenomenon, it was first a vision in the heart of a businessman in Arabia.

Muhammad ibn Abdallah[6] was born in A.D. 570 in the town of Mecca, a thriving trading town near the Red Sea coast of modern-day Saudi Arabia. The Arabian Peninsula comprises 1 million square miles, nearly one-third the size of the United States or Europe. The Arabs of his day occupied this land in tribal societies: Several related families made up a clan, and a cluster of several clans made up a tribe. Each clan was led by an elder (the *majli*); the *majlis* elected one of their own as their chief (*shaykh*). He then led the tribe with their counsel.

The millennium before Muhammad's birth witnessed a repetitive cycle in the Arab world. Farmers would prosper, building towns and villages; a leader would consolidate these urban centers, expanding them into an empire or kingdom; a tribe of nomads would conquer the monarch, seizing his people's possessions and destroying his empire; and the process would begin again. As we will see, this pattern of tribal warfare played a significant role in the beginnings of Islam and helps explain the mindset of radical Muslims today.

Muhammad's world was dominated by two rival superpowers engaged in their own Cold War. To the west stood the Byzantine Empire—heirs of the Roman Empire, now Christianized and foundering in their Dark Ages. To the east stood the Sassanid Empire—heirs of Persia and monarchs of modern-day Iran, Iraq, and regions eastward to the Himalayas. In between lay the Arabian Peninsula, home to autonomous tribes locked in perpetual competition and conflict.

Numerous Jewish tribes lived among them, descended from Hebrews driven out of Palestine by the Romans. In Mecca, a hundred different pagan deities were worshiped. People venerated the seven planets, the moon, and the stars. Many honored family household gods and various angels. Others were engaged in fire worship, a practice contributed by the Magis from Persia. A heretical version of Christianity was also present in the culture. Pilgrims who visited the numerous temples of the land were a mainstay of the local economy.

Muhammad's father, Abd-Allah, was part of the Quraysh, the most powerful tribe in Mecca. He was impoverished, however, and died before his son was born. Muhammad's mother, Amina, died when he was only six. He lived with his grandfather Abdul-Muttalib, who gave him his name. (*Muhammad* means "the Praised One.") After his grandfather's death, Muhammad came to live with his uncle, Abu Talib.

Since his family was very poor, Muhammad was unable to receive a formal education. As a young boy he traveled with his uncle's merchant caravans to far-off nations. Here he may have met Christian monks and heard the stories and teachings of the Bible.

Mecca stands at the crossroads of trade routes between the Indian Ocean and the Mediterranean. In this bustling commercial center, Muhammad soon made a reputation for himself as an honest businessman—he was known as *al-Amin*, "the trusted one." In his early 20s, he was hired by a wealthy widow named Khadija to manage her business and caravans. After three years, when Muhammad was 25 years old, the two were married. Though polygamy was common in their culture, Muhammad married no other wives until Khadija died 25 years later.

This alliance made him a wealthy and prosperous businessman in his own right. The couple had two sons and four daughters, but only their daughter Fatima survived her father. She would eventually marry Ali, Muhammad's younger cousin.

Meeting Gabriel

For years, Muhammad retreated to a cave on the summit of Mount Hira during Ramadan (the ninth month on their calendar) to pray and fast.

During Ramadan in 610, at the age of 40, he was meditating in this cave. On the 17th day of the month, he was gripped by an experience that marked him for the rest of his life and birthed a global movement. Muslims call this event "the Night of Power and Excellence." Tamim Ansary, a Muslim historian, describes the epochal moment this way:

> It was apparently an oral and personal interaction, which started when Muhammad, meditating in the utter darkness of the cave, sensed an overwhelming and terrifying presence: someone else was in the cave with him. Suddenly he felt himself gripped from behind so hard he could not breathe. Then came a voice, not so much heard as felt throughout his being, commanding him to "recite!" Muhammad managed to gasp out that he could not recite.
> The command came again: "Recite!"
> Again Muhammad protested that he could not recite, did not know *what* to recite, but the angel—the voice—the impulse—blazed once more: "Recite!" Thereupon Muhammad felt words of terrible grandeur forming in his heart and the recitation began:
> *Recite in the name of your Lord Who created,*
> *Created humans from a drop of blood.*
> *Recite!*
> *And your Lord is most Bountiful.*
> *He who taught humans by the pen,*
> *taught humans that which they knew not.*
>
> Muhammad came down from the mountain sick with fear, thinking he might have been possessed by a jinn, an evil spirit. Outside he felt a presence filling the world to every horizon. According to some accounts, he

saw a light with something like a human shape within it, which was only more thunderous and terrifying. At home, he told Khadija what had happened, and she assured him that he was perfectly sane, that his visitor had really been an angel, and that he was being called into service by God. "I believe in you," she said, thus becoming Muhammad's first follower.[7]

Of all the deities worshiped by his people, Allah was believed to be the creator God and was thought to have sons and daughters. It was revealed to Muhammad that Allah (Arabic for "the God") is the only true God and that all other deities are false and must be rejected. (Note that Muhammad's father's name, Abd-Allah, means "slave of Allah.") As a descendant of Abraham through Ishmael and his son Kedar, Muhammad felt that this message placed him in the monotheistic line of his ancestor.

Reaction in his hometown

At first Muhammad shared his new message only with his friends and family. Two years later he went public, calling people around Mecca to repent of their polygamy and idolatry and to serve the cause of justice and righteousness. He considered his message to be a continuation of the truth that God had long been delivering to humanity. (Islamic tradition would later claim that God had sent 124,000 prophets to mankind, a number that suggests infinity.)

However, many in his polytheistic culture viewed his monotheistic message as scandalous and even heretical. Even worse, he claimed the most venerated shrine in their culture for his new religion.

In Mecca there is a large square-shaped structure called the *Ka'ba* ("the cube"), measuring 36 feet by 42 feet and standing 43 feet high. Originally dedicated to Hubal, a Nabatean deity, it is covered by a black and gold silk curtain. The Black Stone, a meteor that fell from heaven to earth, is situated in its eastern corner. Local tradition claimed that Adam originally built this structure but it fell into disrepair, so Abraham and Ishmael reconstructed it (Qur'an 2:127).

Muhammad's tribe, the Quraysh, was in charge of the *Ka'ba* and the pilgrimages that thousands made to it each year. By his time it had been dedicated to 360 idols, perhaps representing the days of the year. Muhammad began proclaiming his message that there is only one God and claimed this prestigious shrine for Allah's worship alone. Reaction to Muhammad's proclamations was immediate and vociferous. Business leaders were threatened by his rejection of the religious tourism that resulted from Mecca's polygamy. Followers of the various gods accused him of blasphemy.

For 12 years, as opposition to his movement mounted, Muhammad continued his proclamations in Mecca. He found support from Abu Bakr, a wealthy and influential member of the Quraysh, and his wife and small band of loyal followers.

During this difficult time, the Prophet's response to his opponents was to seek cooperation and practice forbearance, an example often cited by those who view Islam as a peaceful religion.[8] As we will note in chapter 4, many of the Qur'anic verses that counsel tolerance of other religions come from this period of Muhammad's life and work.

Establishing the *Ummah*

A.D. 622 was a pivotal year in Islamic history. Muhammad's wife Khadija had already died, as had his uncle and defender, Abu Talib. Seven elders in his own tribe conspired to have him killed. Muhammad planned a retreat to Yathrib, an agricultural city 280 miles to the north whose elders had already invited him to help them settle tribal disputes.

While waiting for Allah's command to flee, Muhammad dreamed that he was transported from the *Ka'ba* in Mecca to Jerusalem's Holy Temple and then into heaven, where he met Jesus and Abraham and received instructions from Allah. He was then returned to his bed in Mecca. Some Muslims believe this to have been a physical journey, while others view it as a spiritual experience. Called the Night Journey (*Mi'raj*), it is vital for understanding the Muslim commitment to Jerusalem and their Dome of the Rock, as we will see in chapter 5.

Muhammad and his best friend, Abu Bakr, then slipped out of Mecca and hid from his enemies in a cave. Muslim tradition holds that a spider built its web across the mouth of the cave to conceal them. The two then made their way to Yathrib. The city was eventually renamed Medina, meaning "city of the Prophet."

Other followers of Muhammad, some 70 families in all, eventually joined him. This "flight to Medina" is known as the *Hijra* ("severing of ties"). It marks the beginning of the Muslim community, the *Ummah*, and is the first year of the Islamic calendar (subsequent dates are listed as A.H., *anno hegirae*). Muslims believe that their Prophet and his followers were divinely protected from their enemies so they could establish their community together. This foundational event is analogous for Muslims to the Exodus for Jews and the Resurrection for Christians.

Defending his people

Within his first year in Medina, Muhammad's approach toward his opponents changed from the tolerant posture he exhibited in Mecca. Let's set out the facts of this chapter in the Prophet's story, then consider the ways they have been interpreted by orthodox and radical Muslims.

As we noted earlier, tribal warfare was a fact of life in Arab society. In a land with scarce natural resources, trading caravans from distant countries were an important source of revenue. Protecting one's posses- sions while stealing from others was common in their culture.

Within two years of its establishment in Medina, Muhammad's *Ummah* faced economic distress. His migrants from Mecca were traders now living in an agricultural community where they possessed neither the skills nor the land to prosper. What were they to do?

The Prophet soon received a revelation that answered their dilemma: "To those against whom War is made, permission is given (to fight), because they are wronged; and verily, God is Most Power- ful for their aid" (22:39). Muhammad's followers were now permitted to launch attacks against their adversaries in Mecca. Why? Because "(They are) those who have been expelled from their homes in defiance of right, (For no cause) except That they say, 'Our Lord Is God'" (22:40). In other words, the financial distress Muhammad's followers faced was the fault of enemies in Mecca who exiled them from their homes and possessions.

Note that this permission to engage in self-defense extended to non-Muslims as well. The verse continues: "Did not God check one set of people by means of another, there would surely have been pulled down monasteries, churches, synagogues, and mosques, in which the name of God is commemorated in abundant measure." In summary, "God will certainly aid those who aid His (cause); for verily God is Full of Strength, Exalted in Might, (Able to enforce His Will)."

Attacking their enemies

His most famous early biographer, Ibn Ishaq (705-754) states that "the apostle prepared for war in pursuance of God's command to fight his enemies and to fight those polytheists who were near at hand whom God commanded him to fight. This was thirteen years after his call."[9]

Muhammad began by sending men out from Medina to capture booty from Meccan caravans. They conformed to the accepted practice of abstaining from conflict during the four sacred months of the Arab calendar:

> The number of months in the sight of God is twelve (in a year)—so ordained by Him the day He created the heavens and the earth; of them four are sacred: that is the straight usage. So wrong not yourself therein, and fight the Pagans all together as they fight you all together. But know that God is with those who restrain themselves" (9:36).

But when one of his raiding parties attacked a caravan on the last day of Rajab, one of the sacred months, the Prophet received further revelation authorizing such warfare:

> They ask thee concerning fighting in the Prohibited Month. Say: "Fighting therein is a grave (offense); but graver is it in the sight of God to prevent access to the Sacred Mosque, and drive out its members. Tumult and oppression are worse than slaughter" (2:217).

Since Muhammad's enemies in Mecca prohibited his followers' access to the *Ka'ba* and exiled them, war against them even in the sacred months was now authorized.

Their most significant raid was planned against a large caravan from Mecca. Its leader learned of Muhammad's ambush and avoided it, but the Prophet's own Quraysh tribe sent a thousand soldiers against him. The two armies met in the Valley of Badr on the 17th day of Ramadan, A.D. 624, where Muhammad's army of 350 defeated their much larger enemy. Only

14 Muslims died, while 49 of the Meccan army were killed. To Muhammad and his followers, this surprising victory proved that Allah was blessing their movement.

Muhammad knew that his powerful enemies in Mecca would soon retaliate. Upon his return to Medina, the Prophet worked with the city elders to establish a legal document that provided religious freedom for the various tribes within their city and pledged them to defend their community from enemies.

His forces lost a second battle at Uhud but defeated their enemies after a long siege of Medina known as the Battle of the Moat. These victories turned Islam into a movement with military and social strategies. Converts joined *Dar al-Islam*, "the realm of submission to God," in contrast to those who remained in *Dar al-Harb*, "the realm of war."

During these years the Prophet had begun taking wives. As we noted, Muhammad remained monogamous so long as his first wife, Khadija, was alive. After her death he was married to 'Ayisha, the daughter of his best friend, Abu Bakr. She was seven years old when they were betrothed, and nine or ten when their marriage was consummated.

The Prophet then married additional wives, approximately one per year. Some were widows of men who had died in battle for him, while others strengthened political relationships. In total, he married 11 women and had two concubines. While Allah gave him special permission to marry so many women (33:50), revelation soon specified that other Muslim men would be limited to four wives:

> If ye fear that ye shall not be able to deal justly with the orphans, marry women of your choice, two, or three, or four; but if ye fear that ye shall not be able to deal justly (with them). Then only one, or (a captive) that your right hands possess. That will be more suitable, to prevent you from doing injustice (4:3).[10]

Dealing with the Jews

When Muhammad began proclaiming his revelations from Allah, he expected Jews living in Arabia to accept his message and initially taught his followers to pray toward Jerusalem. When the Jews rejected his message, he instructed Muslims to turn their backs on Jerusalem by praying toward Mecca.

Some 20 Jewish tribes lived in Medina before Muhammad's arrival. The three largest and most influential were the Qaynuqa', the Nadir, and the Qurayzah. Each depended financially on their relations with the Quraysh tribe in Mecca. Soon after the Battle of Badr, the Qaynuqa' rebelled against his leadership and were expelled from Medina.

Following his loss at Uhud, Muhammad faced further opposition from the Nadir. After they attempted a failed assassination attempt against the Prophet, they were expelled from the city as well and quickly aligned with Muhammad's enemies.

During the Battle of the Moat, the Qurayzah conspired with opposition forces from Mecca. When the Muslims were once again victorious, the Qurayzah asked permission to leave the city as had the Qaynuqa' and the Nadir. Muhammad refused, believing that they would join his enemies in staging further attacks on his people.

After they were found guilty of treason, approximately 800 Jewish men were beheaded in the public square, and the women and children of the tribe were exiled. Many historians see this initial conflict as a significant source of the enmity that exists between many Muslims and Jews to this day.

Conquering Mecca

In A.D. 628, Muhammad returned to Mecca as a pilgrim. Two years later, he brought an army of 10,000 to the city. Some historians state that the city submitted to his leadership without a fight.[11] However, his earliest biographer tells the story differently. According to Ibn Ishaq, Muhammad ordered fighters loyal to him to slaughter the soldiers of the Quraysh, his own tribe, in punishment for their rejection of his movement. In fact, his division carried a special flag into Mecca, black with a single word written in Arabic: *punishment*.[12]

Muhammad then destroyed the idols in the *Ka'ba* and declared it to be the holiest place on earth. Most of the city converted to Islam. The Prophet exhorted the people to treat each other equally and with respect and announced that he was the last of God's messengers so that no further revelation would come to humanity:

> Today your religion is completed, and the grace of God is fulfilled in your life. And I bear witness that Islam is your religion. O Muslim people, you are prohibited to shed blood among yourselves or to steal from each other or take advantage of each other or to steal the women or wives of other Muslims.
>
> After today there will no longer be two religions existing in Arabia. I descended by Allah with the sword in my hand, and my wealth will come from the shadow of my sword. And the one who will disagree with me will be humiliated and persecuted.[13]

Now that he controlled both Mecca and Medina, the Prophet began to expand his influence and religion across the rest of the Arabian Peninsula.

The death of the Prophet

On June 8, 632, Muhammad laid his head in the lap of his wife 'Ayisha, the daughter of his longtime friend Abu Bakr, and died. According to Muslim tradition, Muhammad's followers dug his grave on this spot and buried him. A mosque was later constructed over the grave and became a place of pilgrimage; it is known today as "the Prophet's Mosque."

Muslims deeply revere their founding Prophet. Many seek to emulate his life as much as possible. When they speak or write his name, they follow it immediately with the words, "Peace Be Upon Him" (sometimes shortened in written form to PBUH).

One Muslim scholar described him in terms that all Muslims would affirm:

> Muhammad is the most favored of mankind, the most honored of all apostles, the prophet of mercy, the head or Imam of the faithful, the bearer of banner of praise, the intercessor, the holder of high position, the possessor of the River of Paradise, under whose banner the sons of Adam will be on the Day of Judgment. He is the best of prophets, and his nation is the best of nations . . . and his creed the noblest of creeds. . . . He was perfect in intellect, and was of noble origin. He had an absolutely graceful form, complete generosity, perfect bravery, excessive humility, useful knowledge . . . perfect fear of God and sublime piety. He was the most eloquent and the most perfect of mankind in every variety of perfection.[14]

Within a single decade, A.D. 622-632, Muhammad united the nomadic tribes of the Arabian Peninsula into a single cohesive nation; gave them a monotheistic faith in place of their polytheistic, tribal religions; organized a powerful society and state; and launched a worldwide movement.

Was Muhammad a man of peace or a radical Muslim?

Would Muhammad have affirmed the two tenets of radical Islam? We begin our discussion with the Prophet's treatment of the Jewish population in Medina, remembering that Muhammad exiled two tribes, then executed the men and exiled the women and children of a third. Armstrong provides a sympathetic interpretation of his treatment of the Qurayzah after the Battle of the Moat:

> The incident marks the nadir of Muhammad's career. It is, however, important to note that the Qurayzah were not killed on religious or racial grounds. None of the other Jewish tribes in the oasis either objected or attempted to intervene, clearly regarding it as a purely political and tribal matter. A significant number of the Arab tribe of Kilab, the clients of Qurayzah, were also executed alongside the Jews. Muhammad had no ideological quarrel with the Jewish people. He once said, "He who wrongs or destroys a Jew or a Christian will have me to answer on the Day of Judgment." The men of Qurayzah were executed for treason. The seventeen other Jewish tribes of Medina remained in the oasis, living on friendly terms with the Muslims for many years, and the Qur'an continued to insist that Muslims remember their spiritual kinship with the People of the Book . . .
>
> Later in the Islamic empires, Jews would enjoy full religious liberty and anti-Semitism would not become a Muslim vice until the Arab/Israeli conflict became acute in the mid-twentieth century.[15]

Abraham Sarker tells the story of Muhammad's relations with the Jewish tribes in Medina differently. After the battles of Badr and Uhud, "a serious division developed between Muhammad and the Jewish community. Muhammad began threatening the Jews. Many Jews died as a result of this conflict, and much of the rest of the Jewish population was expelled under the pretext of breaching the city covenant." He notes that "disdain for the Jewish people" was reflected in the Qur'an: "Strongest among men in enmity to the Believers wilt thou find the Jews and Pagans" (5:82); "Those who reject (Truth) among the People of the Book and among the Polytheists, will be in Hell-fire, to dwell therein (for aye). They are the worst of creatures" (98:6).[16] In chapter 4 we will note several other anti-Semitic passages in the Qur'an.

Don Richardson, a longtime missionary who has written on many world religions, places Muhammad's dealings with the Jews in their worst light. He reports that the Prophet presided personally over the beheading of the men of the Qurayzah and states that their wives and daughters became sex slaves for Muslim men while their boys were sold.[17]

A second issue concerns individuals who opposed the Prophet. Muhammad's earliest biographer, Ibn Ishaq, reports that Muhammad ordered the execution of an elderly Jewish enemy, Ka'b b. al-Ashraf. After Muhammad's victory at the Battle of Badr, al-Ashraf "began to inveigh against the apostle and to recite verses in which he bewailed the Quraysh who were thrown into the pit after having been slain at Badr." He also "composed amatory verses of an insulting nature about the Muslim women." Muhammad asked who would rid him of this man; one of his followers agreed to kill al-Ashraf but needed to lure him from his home through trickery. The Prophet approved this strategy, and the man was soon executed: "I thrust [my dagger] into the lower parts of his body, then I bore down upon it until I reached his genitals, and the enemy of God fell to the ground."[18]

The Battle of Khaybar in 629 illustrates the contradictory nature of Muhammad's relations with his enemies. The Prophet led this attack in response to hostilities incited against him by the Nadir, one of the Jewish tribes he earlier expelled from Medina for treason. During the siege, his followers arrested a Jewish man named Kinana b. al-Rabi', who "had custody of the treasure." When he refused to tell them its location, "the apostle gave orders to al-Zubnayr b. al-'Awwam, 'Torture him until you extract what he has,' so he kindled a fire with flint and steel on his chest until he was nearly dead. Then the apostle delivered him to Muhammad b. Maslama and he struck off his head, in revenge for his brother."

However, when the people of Khaybar surrendered to him, "they asked him to let them go, and spare their lives, and he did so." When the inhabitants of a nearby city "heard what had happened they sent to the apostle asking him to let them go and to spare their lives and they would leave him their property, and he did so."[19]

When a man named Abu 'Afak composed a poem criticizing Muhammad, "the apostle said, 'Who will deal with this rascal for me?'" whereupon a follower "went forth and killed him."[20] After his death, a woman composed a poem criticizing Muhammad's action. The Prophet responded:

> When the apostle heard what she had said he said, "Who will rid me of Marwan's daughter?" 'Umayr b. 'Adiy al-Khatmi who was with him heard him, and that very night he went to her house and killed her. In the morning he came to the apostle and told him what he had done and he said, "You have helped God and His apostle, O 'Umayr!" When he asked if he would have to bear any evil consequences the apostle said, "Two goats won't butt their heads about her," so 'Umayr went back to his people.[21]

How are we to view these actions in light of radical Islam? Remember the two tenets of militant Muslims: (1) Muslims must take up arms to protect Islam from Western aggression, and (2) all citizens of the Western world are enemies of Islam. In the mind of Usama bin Laden and other militant Muslims, any attack against a Muslim constitutes an attack on all Muslims. Defending Islam requires armed aggression against all such foes, including any who support their assault on Muslims.

It is obviously possible to use the life of Muhammad to make a case for this interpretation of Islam. It is also possible to interpret his life as a repudiation of radical Islam.

Militant Muslims would illustrate their first thesis by pointing to Muhammad's attacks against his enemies. In their view, when he initiated conflict with his Meccan opponents, raiding their peaceful caravans and eventually conquering their city, he modeled armed aggression as a defense of Islam. To support their second thesis, they would cite the Prophet's treatment of his enemies and the families of his Jewish opponents.

Those who claim that Muhammad would reject Usama bin Laden's version of Islam could support their thesis by citing the Prophet's life as well. In this view, his raids on Meccan caravans were a convention of seventh-century Arabia, not a model for all cultures and times. He exiled his Jewish opponents rather than executing them until their treason threatened the future of the *Ummah* itself. Individuals who slandered him constituted a threat against the unity and future of Islam. But those who were willing to live at peace with him were permitted to do so.

In much the same manner that the Jews were required to execute the Canaanites lest they lead Israel into sin and ruin (cf. Joshua 6-7), Muhammad was forced to deal harshly with his enemies to preserve the *Ummah*. But his conciliatory posture during his time in Mecca and his constitution endorsing religious tolerance in Medina are examples that transcend the seventh century and are models for Islamic relations with the West today.

Conclusion

Was Muhammad a man of peace in Mecca who became a warmonger in Medina, so that "this soft lamb turned into a roaring lion"?[22] Or did he do what was necessary to defend his people and movement from their enemies?

Two verses, believed to have been revealed to the Prophet near the very end of his life, place our conflicting answers in sharp contrast. The most famous Qur'anic verse regarding peace is this statement: "If any one slew a person—unless it be for murder or for spreading mischief in the land—it would be as if he slew the whole people: and if any one saved a life, it would be as if he saved the life of the whole people" (5:32).

However, the next verse states:

> The punishment of those who wage war against God and His Apostle, and strive with might and main for mischief through the land is: execution, or crucifixion, or the cutting off of hands and feet from opposite sides, or exile from the land: that is their disgrace in this world, and a heavy punishment is theirs in the Hereafter (5:33).

Which verse best expresses the Qur'an's position on radical Islam? For answers, we turn next to an exploration of Islam's holy book.

ENDNOTES

1. Karen Armstrong, *Muhammad: A Prophet for Our Time* (New York: HarperOne, 2007) 6.

2. Wafa Sultan, *A God Who Hates* (New York: St. Martin's Press, 2009) 212.

3. My purpose in this chapter is not to provide an exhaustive biography of Muhammad but to explore the degree to which his life supports the tenets of radical Islam. There are many good biographies of Muhammad and expositions of Islam that introduce readers to his story. Among them: Karen Armstrong, *Islam: A Short History* (New York: The Modern Library, 2002); Armstrong, *Muhammad: A Prophet for Our Time*; John L. Esposito, *Islam: The Straight Path* (New York: Oxford University Press, 1988); Bernard Lewis, *The Crisis of Islam: Holy War and Unholy Terror* (New York: Random House, 2004); Abraham Sarker, *Understand My Muslim People* (Newberg, Oregon: Barclay Press, 2004); and especially Tamim Ansary, *Destiny Disrupted: A History of the World Through Islamic Eyes* (New York: Public Affairs, 2009). Ansary's retelling of world history as a Muslim is an invaluable reference for understanding Islamic history and worldview. For instance, he observes that the phrase "Middle East" assumes that we are standing in Western Europe; if you're standing in China, the "Middle East" is the "Middle West." Ansary prefers to call the region "the Middle World," as it stands between the Mediterranean and Chinese worlds (p. 3).

4. In addition to the works cited above, other sources for this chapter include: Mark A. Gabriel, *Jesus and Muhammad: Profound Differences and Surprising Similarities* (Lake Mary, Florida: Charisma House, 2004); Don Richardson, *Secrets of the Koran* (Ventura, California: Regal, 2003); Anis A. Shorrosh, *Islam Revealed: A Christian Arab's View of Islam* (Nashville, Tennessee: Thomas Nelson Publishers, 1988); and Robert Spencer, *Religion of Peace? Why Christianity Is and Islam Isn't* (Washington, D.C.: Regnery, 2007).

5. Ansary xvii.

6. As noted in chapter 1, "Muhammad" is spelled in a variety of ways across the literature. Some transliterate the Prophet's Arabic name as Mohammed, others as Mohamed, others as Muhamed. I have chosen to use the most popular spelling of the Prophet's name and have standardized its use in the various sources I cite.

7. Ansary 19-20.

8. Note: My reference to Muhammad as "the Prophet" is made out of respect for Muslims' veneration for the founder of their faith. It is not intended to validate their claim that he was a true prophet of God.

9. Ibn Ishaq, *The Life of Muhammad: A Translation of Ishaq's Sirat Rasul Allah*, trans. A. Guillaume (New York: Oxford University Press, 2011 [1955]) 280.

10. Ali notes, "As this condition [requiring fairness to all four wives] is most difficult to fulfill, I understand the recommendation to be towards monogamy" (p. 179).

11. Cf. Armstrong, *Islam* 23.

12. Gabriel 60.

13. Ibn Hisham, *The Life of Muhammad*, 3d. ed., vol. 3, pt. 6 (Beirut, Lebanon: Dar-al-Jil, 1998), p. 8; translated by Gabriel 64-5.

14. Quoted in Sarker 35.

15. Armstrong, *Muhammad* 150-1.

16. Sarker 54.

17. Richardson 50.

18. Ibn Ishaq, 365, 367, 368.

19. Ibid., 515.

20. Ibid., 675.

21. Ibid., 676.

22. Gabriel 49.

CHAPTER FOUR

DOES THE QUR'AN MANDATE VIOLENCE?
ISLAM'S HOLY BOOK AND RADICAL MUSLIMS

A week after 9/11, President George W. Bush made a speech at the Islamic Center of Washington, D.C. in which he stated, "The face of terror is not the true face of Islam. That's not what Islam is about. Islam is peace."[1]

The Web site Al-Islami.com, often cited as an authoritative source on Muslim beliefs, agrees: "Islam is in fact a religion that promotes peace and understanding among people of all faiths, and it strongly prohibits all forms of violence and aggression against all people regardless of their faith or race."[2]

By contrast, three years before 9/11, Usama bin Laden issued this *fatwa* (legal pronouncement):

> In compliance with God's order, we issue the following fatwa to all Muslims: The ruling to kill the Americans and their allies—civilians and military—is an individual duty for every Muslim who can do it in any country in which it is possible to do it. . . . This is in accordance with the words of Almighty God: "and fight the pagans all together as they fight you all together," and "fight them until there is no more tumult or oppression, and there prevail justice and faith in God."[3]

Al Qaeda spokesman Suleiman Abu Gheith elaborated:

> We have the right to kill four million Americans—two million of them children—and to exile twice as many and wound and cripple hundreds of thousands. Furthermore, it is our right to fight them with chemical and biological weapons, so as to afflict them with the fatal maladies that have afflicted the Muslims because of the [Americans'] chemical and biological weapons.[4]

Which is the proper expression of Islam? Let's take our question to the Muslim holy book. Does the Qur'an teach a religion of tolerance, or does it mandate radical Islam?

Jihad and Muhammad

Muhammad's early struggles forged in Islam a commitment to *jihad*, which means "to struggle." This much-debated word can be used in five ways:

- "*Jihad* of the heart," advancing Islam through personal purity.
- "*Jihad* of the mouth," advancing Islam through apologetic argument and poetic literature.
- "*Jihad* of the pen," advancing Islam through writing.
- "*Jihad* of the hand," advancing Islam through good deeds.
- "*Jihad* of the sword," advancing Islam through warfare.

The last category is expressed 109 times in the Qur'an, one out of every 55 verses in Islam's holy book.[5] Some Muslims claim that these references should be interpreted metaphorically. Others believe that the military context of these verses requires that they be understood in military terms. Radical Muslims certainly view them this way, finding in the "sword verses" a mandate to militant action.

In interpreting the Qur'an, it is vital to categorize its teachings chronologically. As we have seen, the book is organized from longest chapters to shortest rather than sequentially. However, its teachings reflect clearly the period in which they were revealed. Of the 114 *suras* in the Qur'an, 86 are classified as Meccan (revealed during the Prophet's work in Mecca) while 28 are Medinian (revealed after the *hijra*).

During the time Muhammad was establishing Islam in Mecca, revelation given to him emphasized persuasion through peaceful means. When he moved to Medina and established the first *Ummah*, he received revelation that authorized fighting to defend Muslims. As he enlarged his movement across the Arabian Peninsula, he received further revelation that mandated conflict to expand Islam. Non-militant Muslims emphasize the teachings found in the first period of his work; radical Muslims emphasize those revelations found in the second and especially the third eras of his leadership.

Advancing Islam peacefully

During the first 12 years of Muhammad's work, his movement met much opposition in Mecca and was forced to proceed through personal persuasion. During this period, the Prophet received several revelations that advocate tolerance and cooperation with non-Muslims.

The most famous is this exhortation: "Let there be no compulsion in religion: Truth stands out clear from Terror: whoever rejects Evil and believes in God hath grasped the most trustworthy hand-hold, that never breaks. And God heareth and knoweth all things" (2:256).

Early in his Meccan work, Muhammad announced this revelation:

> Say: O ye that reject Faith! I worship not that which ye worship, Nor will ye worship that which I worship. And I will not worship that which ye have been wont to worship, Nor will ye worship that which I worship. To you be your Way, and to me mine (109:1-6).

The Prophet revealed that Muslims, Jews, and Christians would all receive rewards in heaven:

> Those who believe (in the Qur'an), and those who follow the Jewish (scriptures), and the Christians and the Sabians [Gnostics], any who believe in God and the Last Day, and work righteousness, shall have their reward with their Lord: on them shall be no fear, nor shall they grieve (2:62).

He said of Christians, "amongst these are men devoted to learning and men who have renounced the world, and they are not arrogant" (5:82). Another statement, given in the "Middle Meccan period"[6] before

Muhammad fled to Medina and established a more warlike posture with non-Muslims, teaches:

> Dispute ye not with the People of the Book, except with means better (than mere disputation), unless it be with those of them who inflict wrong (and injury); but say, "We believe in the Revelation which has come down to us and in that which came down to you; our God and your God is One; and it is to Him that we bow (in Islam)." And thus (it is) that We have sent down the Book to thee. So the People of the Book believe therein, as also do some of these (Pagan Arabs): and none but Unbelievers reject Our Signs (29:46-47).

How are Muslims to deal with those who reject their faith? One of the earliest texts in the Qur'an states: "Have patience with what they say, and leave them with noble (dignity). And leave Me (alone to deal with) those in possession of the good things of life, who (yet) deny the Truth; and bear with them for a little while" (73:10-11). One of the most conciliatory statements in the Qur'an is this verse from the Meccan period:

> Call (them to the Faith) and stand steadfast as thou art commanded, nor follow thou their vain desires; but say: "I believe in the Book which God has sent down; and I am commanded to judge justly between you. God is our Lord and your Lord: For us (is the responsibility for) our deeds, and for you for your deeds. There is no contention between us and you. God will bring us together, and to Him is (Our) final goal" (42:15).

Another early verse exhorts Muslims to "leave them alone until they encounter that Day of theirs, wherein they shall (perforce) swoon (with terror)" (52:45).

If those sections of the Qur'an that were revealed in Mecca were the only revelation given to Muhammad, it is likely that my book on radical Islam would not have been needed. Islam would have taken its place among the world's religions by contending for its beliefs through reason and persuasion. It would have provided no warrant for militant aggression against the non-Muslim world.

Defending Islam

However, the Prophet's posture towards non-Muslims would soon change dramatically. Remember that Muhammad's enemies in Mecca sought his death and exiled his followers. Even after his flight to Medina, he faced opposition from Jewish tribes in Medina and his adversaries in Mecca. During this period, the Prophet received a number of revelations regarding the defense of Islam. Here is the most famous:

> Fight in the cause of God those who fight you, but do not transgress limits; for God loveth not transgressors. And slay them wherever ye catch them, and turn them out from where they have turned you out; for tumult and oppression are worse than slaughter; but fight them not at the Sacred Mosque, unless they (first) fight you there; but if they fight you, slay them. Such is the reward of those who suppress faith. But if they cease, God is Oft-Forgiving, Most Merciful. And fight them on until there is no more tumult or oppression, and there prevail justice and Faith in God, but if they cease, let there be no hostility except to those who practise oppression (2:190-193).

The logic of this text is that Muslims were fighting against enemies who provoked conflict with them. Usama bin Laden made the same claim in his 2002 "Letter to America," beginning with this text:

> To those against whom War is made, permission is given (to fight), because they are wronged; and verily, God is Most Powerful for their aid; (They are) those who have been expelled from their homes in defiance of right, (For no cause) except That they say, "Our Lord Is God" (22:39-40).
>
> Those who believe fight in the cause of God, and those who reject Faith fight in the cause of Evil: so fight ye against the friends of Satan (4:76).

Many self-defensive injunctions are contained in Sura 8 of the Qur'an, titled "*Anfal*, or the Spoils of War." Here we learn that God is at war with unbelievers:

> I will instill terror into the hearts of the Unbelievers: smite ye above their necks and smite all their finger-tips off them. This because they contended against God and His Apostle; if any contend against God and His Apostle, God is strict in punishment. . . . It is not ye who slew them; it was God (8:12-13, 17).

In this conflict with non-Muslims, God gave the victory to Muhammad and his followers:

> Call to mind when ye were a small (band), despised through the land, and afraid that men might despoil and kidnap you; but He provided a safe asylum for you, strengthened you with His aid, and gave you good things for sustenance: that ye might be grateful (8:26).

As a result, safety is found only by accepting Islam:

> Say to the Unbelievers, if (now) they desist (from unbe-
> lief), their past would be forgiven them; but if they persist,
> the punishment of those before them is already (a matter
> of warning for them). And fight them on until there is no
> more tumult or oppression, and there prevail justice and
> faith in God altogether and everywhere; but if they cease,
> verily God doth see all that they do (8:38-39).

Note that in this conflict, Muhammad would receive a fifth of the spoils of war: "And know that out of all the booty that ye may acquire (in war), a fifth share is assigned to God, and to the Apostle, and to near relatives, orphans, the needy, and the wayfarer" (8:41). This would remain his share of future booty, even when his army grew to several thousand soldiers.

All who align with unbelievers are to be defeated: "If ye gain the mastery over them in war, disperse, with them, those who follow them, that they may remember" (8:57). Muslims are to be at peace only with those who seek peace with them: "But if the enemy incline towards peace, do thou (also) incline towards peace, and trust in God: for He is the one that heareth and knoweth (all things)" (8:60).

To summarize: During Muhammad's early period in Medina, rev-elation given to the Prophet authorized self-defense against the enemies of Islam. Moderate Muslims view this revelation as mandating military defense against an enemy who initiates violence against them, but do not believe that it warrants initiatory aggression against non-Muslims.

Conversely, radical Muslims utilize the Qur'anic call to self-defense in justifying their attacks against the West today. As we noted in chapter 2, they claim that the West has been attacking Islam since the Crusades and characterize their militant actions as a defense of the *Ummah*.

Expanding Islam

After securing his community in Medina, the Prophet received a number of revelations that enjoined Muslims to initiate warfare in expanding their movement. At first Allah instructed his followers to abstain from fighting during the four sacred months of their calendar (9:36), but later charged them with fighting for the cause of Islam at any time of the year:

> Fighting is prescribed for you, and ye dislike it. But it is possible that ye dislike a thing which is good for you, and that ye love a thing which is bad for you. But God knoweth, and ye know not. They ask thee concerning fighting in the Prohibited Month. Say: "Fighting therein is a grave (offense); but graver is it in the sight of God to prevent access to the Sacred Mosque, and drive out its members. Tumult and oppression are worse than slaughter. Nor will they cease fighting you until they turn you back from your Faith if they can. And if any of you turn back from their Faith and die in unbelief, their works will bear no fruit in this life and in the Hereafter; they will be Companion of the Fire and will abide therein" (2:216-217).

Sura 9, one of the last chapters given to Muhammad, revealed two years before the Prophet's death, contains many expansionist injunctions. Here we learn that Muslims are to initiate war with all who reject Islam until they convert:

> Fight and slay the pagans wherever ye find them, and seize them, beleaguer them, and lie in wait for them in every stratagem (of war); but if they repent, and establish regular Prayer and practice regular Charity, then open the way for them: for God is Oft-Forgiving, Most Merciful (9:5).

> Fight those who believe not in God nor the Last
> Day, nor hold that forbidden which hath been forbidden
> by God and His Apostle nor acknowledge the Religion of
> truth, (even if they are) of the People of the Book, until
> they pay the *Jizya* with willing submission, and feel them-
> selves subdued (9:29).

Non-Muslims are given three options: convert to Islam, submit to Muslims, and pay the *Jizya* (an annual tax), or die.

Fighting in the cause of Islam is expected of all Muslims:

> Those who believe in God and the Last Day ask thee for
> no exemption from fighting with their goods and persons.
> And God knoweth well those who do their duty. Only
> those ask thee for exemption who believe not in God and
> the Last Day, and whose hearts are in doubt, so that they
> are tossed in their doubts to and fro (9:44-45).

In summary: "O ye who believe! Fight the Unbelievers who gird you about, and let them find firmness in you: and know that God is with those who fear him (9:123).

Moderate Muslims typically interpret these verses as a metaphori-cal call to advance Islam in the world. To radical Muslims, of course, these verses constitute a divine call to aggression against the non-Muslim world.

Reconciling the three views of war

It is clear in the Qur'an that Muhammad's teachings in Mecca coun-seled tolerance and acceptance of other religions, while his exhortations upon founding the *Ummah* in Medina called Muslims to defend Islam and then to initiate conflict with non-Muslims. How do Muslims reconcile these three positions?

Those who advocate initiatory war with non-Muslims utilize the principle of *naskh*—the belief that Muhammad's revelations were progressive, so that latter teachings supersede earlier disclosures. They find this interpretive theory in the Qur'an itself: "None of Our revelations do We abrogate or cause to be forgotten, but We substitute something better or similar" (2:106); "We substitute one revelation for another, and God knows best what he reveals (in stages)" (16:101); "We have revealed it by stages" (17:106).

Sayyid Qutb, whose *Milestones* was a seminal work in the 20th-century evolution of radical Islam, took this position. He explained that during the Meccan period of Muhammad's work, "the Qur'an explained to man the secret of his existence and the secret of the universe surrounding him."[7] While beginning his movement, "the command to refrain from fighting during the Meccan period was a temporary stage in a long journey."[8] But when Muhammad established the *Ummah* in Medina, "permission was given to fight. Then he was commanded to fight those who fought him. . . . Later he was commanded to fight the polytheists until God's religion was fully established."[9]

In this view, moderate verses from the Meccan period have been superseded by militant verses, which call Muslims to defend Islam and to initiate war against non-Muslims. However, it is possible to take a contrary, less aggressive approach to Islam's relationship with the non-Muslim world. Moderate Muslims could view Meccan revelations as God's intention for their relations with the non-Muslim world and turn to self-defense only when necessary. They could interpret expansionist calls to arms as metaphors for advancing Islam or view them as necessary only until the Muslim world was established on the Arabian Peninsula. When Islam built a home and base for its global ministry, such expansionist aggression would no longer be needed or warranted.

Islam and non-Muslims

Some clear Qur'anic teachings regarding non-Muslims seem beyond interpretive dispute; many fuel radical Islam's rejection of Israel and the West. The Qur'an revealed that Muslims are "the best of Peoples, evolved for mankind" (3:110a). By contrast, Muhammad laments: "If only the People of the Book had faith: it were best for them: among them are some who have faith, but most of them are perverted transgressors" (3:110b).

As a result, all non-Muslims are to be avoided: "Shun those who turn away from Our Message and desire nothing but the life of this world" (53:29); "if they hearken not to thee, know that they only follow their own lusts: and who is more astray than one who follows his own lusts, devoid of guidance from God?" (28:50).

Even family members who do not convert to Islam are to be rejected: "Thou wilt not find any people who believe in God and the Last Day, loving those who resist God and His Apostle, even though they were their fathers or their sons, or their brothers, or their kindred" (58:22); "There is for you an excellent example (to follow) in Abraham and those with him, when they said to their people: 'We are clear of you and of whatever ye worship besides God: we have rejected you, and there has arisen, between us and you, enmity and hatred forever,--unless ye believe in God and Him alone'" (60:4).

Muhammad warned his followers that Jews and Christians would seek to lead them away from their new faith: "Quite a number of the People of the Book wish they could turn you (people) back to infidelity after ye have believed" (2:109); "Never will the Jews or the Christians be satisfied with thee unless thou follow their form of religion" (2:120); "O ye who believe! if ye listen to a faction among the People of the Book, they would (indeed) render you apostates after ye have believed!" (3:100); "follow not their vain desires, but beware of them lest they beguile thee from any of that (teaching) which God hath sent down to thee" (5:49).

Jews and Christians are wrong about the afterlife: "Let not the strutting about of the Unbelievers through the land deceive thee; Little is it for enjoyment; their ultimate abode is Hell: what an evil bed (to lie on)!" (3:196-7); "The Day whereon they will issue from their sepulchres in sudden haste as if they were rushing to a goal-post (fixed for them), Their eyes lowered in dejection, ignominy covering them (all over)! Such is the Day the which they are promised!" (70:43-44).

Scorn for Judaism is clearly reflected in the Qur'an:

- "Well ye knew those amongst you who transgressed in the matter of the Sabbath: We said to them: 'Be ye apes, despised and rejected'" (2:65).
- "Those who incurred the curse of God and his wrath, those of whom some he transformed into apes and swine, those who worshipped evil; these are (many times) worse in rank, and far more astray from the even path!" (5:60).
- "Why do not the Rabbis and the doctors of the law forbid them from their (habit of) uttering sinful words and eating things forbidden? Evil indeed are their works" (5:63).
- "Strongest among men in enmity to the Believers wilt thou find the Jews and the Pagans" (5:82).
- "When in their insolence they transgressed (all) prohibitions, We said to them: 'Be ye apes, despised and rejected'" (7:166).

Revelation given during Muhammad's Medinian period makes clear Islam's rejection of Christians as well:

- "They do blaspheme who say: 'God is Christ the son of Mary.' But said Christ: 'O Children of Israel! Worship God, my Lord and your Lord.' Whoever joins other gods with God, God will forbid him the Garden, and the Fire will be his abode. There will for the wrong-doers be no one to help. They do blaspheme who say: God is one of three in a Trinity: for there is no god except One God. If they desist not from their word (of blasphemy), verily a grievous penalty will befall the blasphemers among them" (5:72-73).

- "God's curse be on them: how they are deluded away from the Truth! They take their priests and their anchorites to be their lords in derogation of God, and (they take as their Lord) Christ the son of Mary; yet they were commanded to worship but One God: there is no god but He, Praise and glory to Him: (far is He) from having the partners they associate (with Him)" (9:30-31).
- "And indeed Hell surrounds the Unbelievers (on all sides)" (9:49).
- "Know they not that for those who oppose God and His Apostle, is the Fire of Hell?—Wherein they shall dwell. That is the supreme disgrace" (9:63).
- "No son did God beget, nor is there any god along with him" (23:91).
- "Those who reject (Truth) among the People of the Book and among the Polytheists, will be in Hell-fire, to dwell therein (for aye). They are the worst of creatures" (98:6).

Those who oppose Islam will not be forgiven by God: "Whether thou ask for their forgiveness, or not, (their sin is unforgivable): if thou ask seventy times for their forgiveness, God will not forgive them: because they have rejected God and His Apostle; and God guideth not those who are perversely rebellious" (9:80); "That is their reward, Hell; because they rejected Faith, and took My Signs and My Messengers by way of jest" (18:106).

Muslims should not pray for non-Muslims: "It is not fitting, for the Prophet and those who believe, that they should pray for forgiveness for Pagans, even though they be of kin, after it is clear to them that they are companions of the Fire" (9:113). Note that the Qur'an warns non-Muslims of hell 783 times.[10]

Does the Qur'an's view of non-Muslims mandate violence against them? Again, it is possible to view this issue in two ways. Moderate Muslims could interpret the Qur'anic rejection of non-Muslims as motivation for evangelism, while radical Muslims could view the same verses as justifying military aggression against these enemies of the faith.

The rewards of dying for Islam

The Qur'anic promise of eternal reward for those who die in the service of Islam is a major incentive for radical Muslims. For example, Usama bin Laden cited this text in his 2002 "Letter to America," describing "the Nation that desires death more than you desire life":

> Think not of those who are slain in God's way as dead. Nay, they live, finding their sustenance in the Presence of their Lord; They rejoice in the Bounty provided by God: and with regard to those left behind, who have not yet joined them (in their bliss), the (Martyrs) glory in the fact that on them is no fear, nor have they (cause to) grieve. They glory in the Grace and the Bounty from God, and in the fact that God suffereth not the reward of the Faithful to be lost (in the least) (3:169-71).

After their loss at the battle of Uhud, Muslims received this revelation through their Prophet:

> O ye who believe! Shall I lead you to a bargain that will save you from a grievous Penalty?—That he believe in God and His Apostle, and that ye strive (your utmost) in the Cause of God, with your property and your persons: that will be best for you, if ye but knew! He will forgive you your sins, and admit you to Gardens beneath which Rivers flow, and to beautiful Mansions in Gardens of Eternity: that is indeed the supreme Achievement. And another (favour will He bestow), which ye do love, help from God and a speedy victory. So give the glad Tidings to the Believers (61:10-13).

Many Muslims understand this promise to relate specifically to those who die for the cause of Islam: "that ye strive (your utmost) in the Cause of God, with your property and your persons." In other words, if they die in battle for Islam, they are guaranteed a place in heaven.

The Qur'an offers many such promises of eternal reward for those who die for their Muslim faith:

- "Say not of those who are slain in the way of God: 'They are dead.' Nay, they are living, though ye perceive (it) not" (2:154).
- "If ye are slain, or die in the way of God, forgiveness and mercy from God are far better than all they could amass. And if ye die, or are slain, Lo! it is unto God that ye are brought together" (3:157-158).
- "Those who have left their homes, or been driven out therefrom, or suffered harm in My Cause, or fought

> or been slain—verily I will blot out from them their
> iniquities, and admit them into Gardens with rivers
> flowing beneath; a reward from the Presence of God,
> and from His Presence is the best of rewards" (3:195).

In heaven these martyrs will be rewarded with "(Maidens), chaste, restraining their glances, whom no man or Jinn before them has touched" (55:56). These women are described as "Companions with beautiful, big, and lustrous eyes" (44:54). Some Muslims interpret these promises literally while others view them figuratively.[11]

Note that dying for Islam is the only way a Muslim can be guaranteed of salvation. In the afterlife, God "shall set up scales of justice for the Day of Judgment" (21:47). At that time, "those whose balance (of good deeds) is heavy, they will attain salvation: But those whose balance is light, will be those who have lost their souls, in Hell will they abide. The Fire will burn their faces, and they will therein grin, with their lips displaced" (23:102-4).

As you can imagine, the promise of heavenly reward for earthly martyrdom is a powerful incentive for those who wage war against the West on behalf of Islam.

Conclusion

Sayyid Qutb, one of the most influential voices in the history of radical Islam, based his violent views on the Qur'an:

> The spring from which the Companions of the Prophet—
> peace be on him—drank was the Qur'an; only the Qur'an
> as the *Hadith* of the Prophet and his teachings were off-
> spring of this fountainhead. When someone asked the
> Mother of the Faithful, 'Aisha—may God be pleased with

her, about the character of the Prophet—peace be on him, she answered, 'His character was the Qur'an.'"

The Qur'an was the only source from which they quenched their thirst, and this was the only mold in which they formed their lives. This was the only guidance for them.[12]

Did he interpret Islam's holy book correctly? Is the Qur'an a book of peace or a call to violence? Understanding any body of literature requires "hermeneutics" (principles of interpretation). Let's contrast the hermeneutics of Muslims with those of Christian theologians, taking as our example the Jewish invasion of Canaan.

There is no question that the Lord specifically commanded Joshua to attack Jericho, a fortified city in eastern Canaan, with the result that Israelite soldiers "destroyed with the sword every living thing in it—men and women, young and old, cattle, sheep and donkeys" (Joshua 6:21). Generations later, King Saul lost his kingdom in part because he did not kill King Agag after defeating the Amalekites (1 Samuel 15:1-35).

Do these biblical passages issue a call to violence analogous to a radical Muslim's commitment to advance Islam through aggression? Consider two interpretive facts.

First, the biblical narratives are descriptive, not prescriptive. In other words, they tell us what God told Joshua and Saul to do but do not issue the same instructions to us. These stories are in Scripture to teach principles rather than to transmit commands. In the case of the idolatrous Canaanites and Amalekites, if the Jewish people compromised and cohabited with their enemies they would soon become corrupted by their paganism. The principle they illustrate is that we should never compromise spiritually with sin.

By contrast, the Qur'anic call to defend Islam and to initiate aggression with non-Muslims is issued through direct commands to the reader. This call is not transmitted as historical stories but as clear and timeless injunctions.

Second, Christians read the Old Testament in light of the New Testament, believing that God has revealed himself progressively.[13] While the Hebrew people were required to advance and defend their nation through warfare, Jesus clearly taught his followers to "love your enemies and pray for those who persecute you, that you may be sons of your Father in heaven" (Matthew 5:44-45).

There is not a single New Testament text that calls believers to violence against their opponents. Only once in the New Testament did a Christian take up arms against an enemy: Peter's defense of Jesus in the Garden of Gethsemane. When his disciple cut off the right ear of the high priest's servant, "Jesus answered, 'No more of this!' And he touched the man's ear and healed him" (Luke 22:51).

Many Muslims read the Qur'an progressively as well, judging earlier teachings in light of later revelation. But while the Bible moves from military engagement to non-violent missions and ministry, the Qur'an moves from non-violent engagement in Mecca to military action in Medina. Muhammad's followers conducted 70 raids against their opponents in the Prophet's lifetime; Jesus' followers expanded the Kingdom of God through preaching, teaching, and healing (cf. Matthew 10).

It is plausible to interpret the Qur'an in the way Christians interpret the Bible. We read Old Testament passages regarding violence as principles, but we interpret New Testament commands to forgive our enemies as binding. In the same way, Muslims can read Medinian calls to violence as principles but interpret Meccan calls to tolerance as binding today.

It is also plausible to interpret the Qur'an in the opposite way. Muslims can read Meccan passages regarding non-violence as principles rather than calls to tolerance. And they can interpret Medinian calls to aggression as binding today.

Which approach has characterized Muslims across their history? We turn next to a brief survey of Islam after Muhammad and the rise of radical Islam today.

ENDNOTES

1. http://georgewbush-whitehouse.archives.gov/news/releases/2001/09/20010917-11.html, accessed 29 June 2011.

2. http://www.al-islami.com/islam/religion_of_peace.php, accessed 29 June 2011.

3. http://www.mideastweb.org/osamabinladen2.htm, accessed 29 June 2011.

4. http://www.jewishpost.com/archives/news/why-we-fight-america-al-qaida-spokesman-explains-september-11-and-declares-intentions-to-kill-4-million-americans-with-weapons-of-mass-destruction.html, accessed 3 July 2011.

5. Don Richardson, *Secrets of the Koran* (Ventura, California: Regal Books, 2003) 28.

6. Ali 1028.

7. Sayyid Qutb, *Milestones* (Damascus, Syria: Dar al-Ilm, n.d.) 23.

8. Ibid., 65.

9. Ibid., 53.

10. Richardson 229.

11. Ali offers this interpretive note: "These symbolic words need not be taken to mean that there will be eating and drinking, or dressing or marriage or any physical things of that kind. There will be life, but free from all earthly grossness. The women as well as the men of this life will attain to this indescribable bliss" (p. 1352).

12. Qutb 16.

13. Cf. Gordon D. Fee and Douglas Stuart, *How To Read the Bible For All Its Worth*, 2d ed. (Grand Rapids, Michigan: Zondervan, 1993) 150-4; James C. Denison, *The Bible: You Can Believe It* (Dallas, Texas: BaptistWay Press, 2005) 129-30.

CHAPTER FIVE

WHY DO THEY STILL HATE US?
RADICAL ISLAM'S INDICTMENT OF THE WESTERN WORLD[1]

The face of terror today was born and educated in America. Anwar al-Awlaki was born on April 22, 1971, in Las Cruces, New Mexico. His father, Nasser al-Awlaki, was studying at New Mexico State University on a Fulbright scholarship before earning his Ph.D. at the University of Nebraska. Their family lived in New Mexico, Nebraska, and Minnesota before moving to Yemen when Anwar was seven years old. His father became an agriculture minister, president of Sana'a University, and adviser to Yemen's President Ali Abdullah Saleh. While growing up in Yemen, his son, like so many young Muslims, memorized the Qur'an.

Anwar returned to the States in 1991 to attend Colorado State University. A student of civil engineering, he wore jeans and blended into

American culture. He was elected president of the Muslim Student Association, where he gained a reputation as a centrist.

After 9/11, the FBI interviewed him several times as a source on Islamic radicals. Invited to the Pentagon as part of a Muslim-outreach program, he later led a prayer at the Capitol and was interviewed by PBS. He then completed a master's degree in educational leadership at San Diego State University and did course work for a Ph.D. at George Washington University in Washington, D.C., before returning to Yemen.

There his increasingly radical views came to the attention of government officials, who imprisoned him for nearly two years. During this time he began reading the works of Sayyid Qutb (see chapter 6), which had a major influence on his thinking and actions.

Awlaki is today the most effective recruiter of terrorists in the English-speaking world. His best-known essay is titled "44 Ways to Support Jihad." His radical sermons have a large global following on the Internet. His legacy so far includes Major Nidal Malik Hasan, the man charged with killing 13 people and wounding 32 others at Fort Hood, Texas, on November 5, 2009. This was the worst mass killing on a military base in U.S. history. He and Awlaki had exchanged at least 18 e-mails discussing *Shari'a* justification for killing American soldiers.

Awlaki recruited Umar Farouk Abdulmutallab, the Nigerian who is charged with attempting to blow up Flight 253 on Christmas Day 2009. He influenced Faisal Shahazad, the Pakistani-American man accused of attempting to detonate a car bomb in Times Square.

Awlaki issued a *fatwa* calling for the execution of a *Seattle Weekly* cartoonist after she published a caricature of the Prophet Muhammad. At the suggestion of the FBI she changed her name, moved, and went into hiding. And he was behind the October 2010 attempt to bomb cargo planes flying from Yemen to Chicago.

Awlaki has been designated a global terrorist by the U.S. Treasury Department, an action that blocked his assets and made it a crime for

Americans to engage in transactions with him. The U.S. government has authorized his execution even though he is an American citizen. Three days after U.S. special operations forces killed Usama bin Laden, an American military drone attempted to kill Awlaki in a remote region of Yemen but failed.

What caused this American-born Muslim to turn on his country? What motivated other "homegrown terrorists" to do the same? For 13 centuries, radical Islam was not a significant threat to the West. Why now? What factors fuel radical Muslims today? And why do they hate America so vehemently?

Let's explore the four crimes they allege against the Western world.

Allegation No. 1: We impose non-Islamic governments on the Muslim world.

In his "Letter to America," Usama bin Laden issued this clear challenge: "We call upon you to end your support of the corrupt leaders in our countries. Do not interfere in our politics and method of education. Leave us alone, or else expect us in New York and Washington."[2]

Why did he believe that the West interferes with the politics of the Muslim world? If we do, why would such an imposition constitute an attack on Islam requiring military response against the West?

The rise of the Muslim empire

After the death of Muhammad, his friend and father-in-law Abu Bakr led Islam for 14 years (632 to 646). He was succeeded by Umar ibn al-Khattab, a giant of a man who had been one of Muhammad's fiercest supporters and warriors. Under the leadership of their first two *caliphs* ("successors"), Muslims conquered Jerusalem, Syria, Palestine, Egypt, Persia (modern-day Iran), and Mesopotamia (modern-day Iraq).

Upon Umar's death (he was stabbed by a Persian prisoner of war), he was succeeded by Uthman ibn Affan, Muhammad's fifth cousin. Uthman provided effective financial management for the Muslim movement and instituted significant financial reforms. Not all of these were popular; in the 34th year of the Muslim era, rioters beat him to death. He was succeeded by Ali ibn Abu Talib, the Prophet's son-in-law. In the sixth year of his leadership, Ali was assassinated.

These first four leaders are known as the *Rashidun*, the "Rightly Guided Caliphs." Within a century after the death of Muhammad, the Islamic empire expanded under their leadership westward through North Africa and the Middle East to Southern France and Spain. It also reached eastward throughout Central Asia to the borders of China. In the process, Muslims took in much of the oldest and strongest Christian territory.

The spread of Islam in Western Europe was finally checked by Charles Martel at the Battle of Tours (in France) in 732, exactly a century after the death of Muhammad. Spain was later reclaimed for Christianity, but a wide belt of territory from Morocco to Pakistan and Indonesia remained Muslim and is so today.

Following the *Rashidun*, the *Umayyads* (7th – 8th centuries) and *Abbasids* (8th – 13th centuries) ruled the Muslim world. At their height they controlled a region as large as the Roman Empire. After the Mongol invasion (1206-1324), the Ottoman Empire (1299-1923) rose in Turkey to conquer much of Eastern Europe and nearly the entire Arab world.

The decline of the Muslim empire

Today there is no single Muslim leader and no organized global Islamic movement. How did the Muslim empire fall into its current state of disorder and decline? Why is the West to blame?

The Ottomans aligned with the Central Powers of World War I—Germany, Russia, and Austro-Hungary—and lost their empire when the war ended. After winning the Turkish War for Independence (1919-21), the first president of the Turkish Republic, Mustafa Kemal Ataturk, transferred the powers of Muslim clerical leaders to the Grand National Assembly of Turkey.

On March 3, 1924, he abolished the caliphate, the office by which a single successor to Muhammad had led the Muslim world. Radical Muslims call this act the "mother of all crimes" and aim to reestablish the caliphate. Turkey joined the United Nations in 1945 and became a multi-party state two years later, further Westernizing the country's governance.

Militant Muslims blame the Western world for both the decline of the Muslim empire and the loss of their caliphate. In their minds, the Allies imposed Western political values on the Muslim world after winning the war. They encouraged and aided Western-leaning Muslim leaders such as Ataturk in their refusal to govern according to *Sharia*.

We continue to support monarchies and democracies across the Muslim world. To radical Muslims, the only true Islamic state is one governed solely by *Sharia*. However, monarchies exist today in Bahrain, Brunei, Jordan, Kuwait, Malaysia, Morocco, Oman, Qatar, Saudi Arabia, and the United Arab Emirates. Constitutional democracies govern Pakistan, Turkey and the Philippines. Note that each of these countries is aligned in significant ways with America and the West. Of course, our military displaced the rulers of Afghanistan and Iraq, replacing them with democracies as well.

In each case, Western influence and military power have supported Muslim leaders who refuse to govern solely according to *Sharia*. To radical Muslims, such support constitutes a military attack on Islam that must be answered with military might.

Allegation No. 2: We impose non-Islamic values on the Muslim world.

Muslims remember the days when Islam was unquestionably the leading culture and civilization on earth. Many blame the West for its demise. Bernard Lewis, one of the foremost scholars on Islam writing today, states:

> In the period which European historians see as a dark interlude between the decline of ancient civilization—Greece and Rome—and the rise of modern civilization—Europe, Islam was the leading civilization in the world, marked as such by its great and powerful kingdoms, its rich and varied industry and commerce, its original and creative sciences and letters. Islam, far more than Christendom, was the intermediate stage between the ancient East and the modern West, to which it contributed significantly.[3]

Most Americans do not know that Muslims were the first to develop algebra (from *al-jabr,* an Arabic word that means "restoration") from its Babylonian and Greek roots. Muslim scholars advanced chemistry, astronomy, and mathematics ("Arabic" numbers were adopted from Indian antecedents) and are credited with the discovery of several acids, including acetic, citric, nitric, sulfuric, and hydrochloric. Muslim scholars Avicenna and Averroes transmitted and popularized the works of Aristotle, which had largely been forgotten after the demise of the Roman Empire.

Muslim artists developed illuminated manuscripts, portraiture, woodwork, and ceramics, and advanced the art of calligraphy. Muslim inventors created the first prefabricated homes, the bridge mill, and underarm deodorant. Muslim musicians created the marching band and military band, developed during the Ottoman Empire. And Muslim farmers in 15th-century Yemen were the first people to roast and brew coffee beans.

Today most people do not associate Islam with cultural advance. Why not? Radical Muslims, inspired by two of the most significant intellectuals in Islamic history, are convinced that the fault lies with the West.

Declaring *jihad*: Ibn Taymiyya and true Islam

Few in the West have heard of Taqi al-Din Ibn Taymiyya (1268-1328), but he is to blame for much of the ideology that characterizes radical Islam today.[4] Here's his story in brief.

Islam was born in an agrarian world that fostered conservatism. Until the modern era, farmers produced crops as they had for centuries. They owned a fixed amount of land, which limited the production they could generate. Innovation was irrelevant if not harmful.

Such an environment produces a culture that looks to the past more than to the future. The same can true of the religion that culture embraces. Muslims in the medieval world looked to the Prophet as their guide in all things, wishing to live according to *Shari'a* in all its dimensions. From its inception through the Ottoman Empire, the Muslim world was governed by laws that it had followed for centuries, or at least that was the ideal.

No one was more instrumental in advancing this ideal than Ibn Taymiyya. Born in the ancient town of Harran in modern-day Turkey, his father and grandfather were both theologians. He manifested the traits of a zealot as a young man, overturning backgammon tables and railing against colleagues whose purity of faith he questioned. He was eventually imprisoned in the Citadel of Damascus, where he died.

Ibn Taymiyya was convinced that the clerics of his day were not fully committed to live by *Shari'a* alone. He wanted rulers to consult the *ulema* (religious scholars) on all matters of governance and called for all Muslims to take up arms in expanding the *Ummah* around the world. In fact, he was convinced that armed *jihad* in the cause of Islam was as significant as the five pillars of Islam. He also announced that all who do not govern and live by *Shari'a* alone are apostate and must be killed.

This ideology made Ibn Taymiyya a significant problem for the authorities, until the Mongols arrived. In 1258 these invaders from the east sacked Baghdad, which had been the center of Islamic power for five centuries. Their control over much of the Middle East threw the Muslim world into crisis. Their conversion to Islam only complicated things; how could Arab Muslims go to war against fellow Muslims?

Enter Ibn Taymiyya. For years he had been warning Muslims that they must live only by the Qur'an and the *Hadith*. He was convinced that anyone who did not live solely by *Shari'a* is not a true Muslim, a position that had gotten him into repeated trouble with the rulers of his day.

Now, however, his ideology proved extremely useful. Since the Mongols did not live exclusively by *Shari'a*, they could be characterized as pagans rather than true Muslims. This declaration enabled Arabs to fight against the Mongols, expelling them from their region and eventually reestablishing their Empire under the Ottomans.

Ibn Taymiyya's conviction that only those who live exclusively by *Shari'a* are true Muslims has plagued Islam ever since. As we will see in chapter 6, it was instrumental in forming the worldview of Sayyid Qutb, the most significant ideologue behind radical Islam today. It was used to justify the assassination of Egyptian President Anwar el-Sadat in 1981 and is claimed by radical Muslims in their struggle against any leader or government that does not share their commitment to live by *Shari'a* alone.

Burning books: Abd al-Wahhab and apostasy

Muhammad ibn Abd al-Wahhab (1703-92) was born in the Arabian town of al-Uyaina; his father and grandfather were judges. Like Ibn Taymiyya, Abd al-Wahhab developed an early reputation as a zealot, getting expelled from one seminary after condemning the people for apostasy. In studying the works of Ibn Taymiyya he found a fellow *jihadist* for Islam and began preaching against the lax rulers and practices of his day. He even advocated burning books he found contrary to true Islam and executing those who wrote, copied, or taught them.

Forced by local authorities to flee, he found protection in the village of Dariya under its ruling sheikh, Muhammad ibn Saud. Ibn Saud coupled Abd al-Wahhab's religious fervor with his own passion to unify and reform the people of central Arabia. By his death in 1765, Ibn Saud controlled most of the central Arabian plateau.

His descendants continued their alliance with Abd al-Wahhab and his puritanical followers, forging an alliance that persists today. After the defeat of the Ottoman Empire, the House of Saud, led by Abdul-Aziz bin Saud, created the modern state of Saudi Arabia in 1932. He declared Wahhabi Islam to be the authorized form of Islam in the country.

Fighting the West

What do Ibn Taymiyya and Abd ibn-Wahhab have to do with radical Islam's fight against Western culture today? Both were convinced that the only true Muslim state is one that is governed unconditionally by *Shari'a* and that the only culture that Muslims should embrace is one founded solely on *Shari'a*. When facing invasions from outsiders, Muslims must rebuke and refute their oppressors.

With the decline of the Ottoman Empire and rise of the West, the Muslim world began to interact with a culture it had never confronted before. The discovery of oil on the Arabian Peninsula brought Western governments, companies, and finances to their lands. These outsiders introduced Western values such as the autonomy of the individual, the equality of women, and the separation of church and state. Their moral values especially alarmed many Muslims as the ethical relativism and decadence of the West were exported to their world through books and media.

Radical Muslims see these cultural exports as an attack on Islam. They believe that we oppress their people through our books, movies, television, and music just as we oppress them through our politics and military. The rise of the Internet has made it even easier for us to corrupt their culture with our own.

For example, bin Laden's "Letter to America" calls our nation "the worst civilization witnessed by the history of mankind." He condemns us for "the production, trading and usage of intoxicants," "acts of immorality" that we consider to be "pillars of personal freedom," "gambling in all its forms," "the trade of sex in all its forms," our "industrial waste and gases," and our World War II decision to bomb Japan.

His letter especially criticizes the role of women in our culture: "You are a nation that exploits women like consumer products or advertising tools calling upon customers to purchase them. You use women to serve passengers, visitors, and strangers to increase your profit margins. You then rant that you support the liberation of women."

Ibn Taymiyya and Abd al-Wahhab would agree. They were convinced that any culture that does not live by *Shari'a* alone is not Muslim. Such a culture must be rejected at every turn. If that culture tries to impose its values on the Muslim world it has declared war against Islam and must be attacked and defeated. In other words, American movies had as much to do with 9/11 as our military.

Allegation No. 3: We are "Crusaders."

In 1095, Pope Urban II announced the First Crusade. Four years later the Crusaders conquered Jerusalem. In 1187, Saladin defeated the Crusaders at the battle of Hattin and restored Jerusalem to Islam.

Why do the Crusades still matter to Muslims a thousand years later? To answer this critical question we need to understand the *Ummah*, the "community" of Muslims that transcends geography and time.

In the fractious period following Muhammad's death, his successor Abu Bakr declared that the *Ummah* must be one. As God is whole and single, so his followers must be a single unity. The *Ummah* thus constitutes all Muslims in all countries across all time. Bernard Lewis explains:

> In the Western world, the basic unit of human organization is the nation, in America but not European usage virtually synonymous with country. This is then subdivided in various ways, one of which is by religion. Muslims, however, tend to see not a nation subdivided into religious groups but a religion subdivided into nations.[5]

As a result, what happens to any Muslim happens to all Muslims. By attacking Muslims in 1095, Crusaders launched the first strike against the *Ummah*. By supporting Israel in its conflict with Palestinians (see below), America is attacking all Muslims. This is a critical motivation for those who believe they are defending Islam by attacking us.

This connection with the larger *Ummah* is driving many European Muslims to radicalism as well. Younger Muslims are especially susceptible to the rhetoric that they are members of an imagined global Muslim community, so their local citizenship is unimportant. This supranational identity gives them a sense of belonging and personal significance and connects them to the first Muslims in their *jihad* against their enemies. This time, however, the enemy are the Jews and Crusaders who have invaded the homeland of Islam and continue to oppress and pillage its people.

Radical Muslims find direct historic parallels between the original Crusades and Western actions in the Middle East today. As the first Crusaders attacked Muslims in Israel and Jerusalem, so the United States supports Israel in its perceived aggression against Palestinians today. As the first Crusaders carved out feudal states in the Middle East, so today the West is building nations in Iraq and Afghanistan that are seen as American proxy states. As the first Crusaders and their sponsors profited financially from their invasions, so the West profits today from its relations with Saudi Arabia and other oil-producing Muslim nations.

Note bin Laden's use of "Crusader" language in his letter to America: "If the Americans refuse to listen to our advice and the goodness, guidance and righteousness that we call them to, then be aware that you will lose this Crusade Bush began, just like the other previous Crusades in which you were humiliated by the hands of the Mujahideen, fleeing to your home in great silence and disgrace."[6]

He viewed our presence in the Middle East as a continuation of the Crusades begun a thousand years ago. In his *fatwa* of February 23, 1998, he claims, "for over seven years the United States has been occupying the lands of Islam in the holiest of places, the Arabian Peninsula, plundering its riches, dictating to its rulers, humiliating its people, terrorizing its neighbors, and turning its bases in the Peninsula into a spearhead through which to fight the neighboring Muslim peoples."

He further condemns "their eagerness to destroy Iraq, the strongest neighboring Arab state, and their endeavor to fragment all the states of the region such as Iraq, Saudi Arabia, Egypt, and Sudan into paper statelets and through their disunion and weakness to guarantee Israel's survival and the continuation of the brutal crusade occupation of the Peninsula."[7]

Note his description of our presence in Saudi Arabia as a "crusade occupation." Radical Muslims will never forget the Crusades. To them, an attack against the Muslim world a millennium ago is still an attack on Islam. They view any incursion into the Muslim world today, such as America's presence in Saudi Arabia, Afghanistan, and Iraq, as another example of the "crusader" spirit that must be met with force.

Allegation No. 4: We support the "Zionists."

Muslims believe that Abraham offered Ishmael, not Isaac, to God. This assertion, if true, would mean that Ishmael's Arab descendants, not the Jews, are the true "people of God." As a result, they reject Israel's claim to the Holy Land.

When the Romans put down the Jewish Bar Kochba revolt in A.D. 135, Emperor Hadrian renamed the region "Provincia Syria Palaestina," later shortened to "Palestine." The word is the Latin form of "Philistine," the name of the people living along the Mediterranean coast. (None were Arabs.) The region remained "Palestine" until the birth of the modern state of Israel on May 14, 1948.

America and the West were deeply involved in the creation and defense of this new nation. The first Zionist (from "Zion," a word that refers to Jerusalem) conference was held in Basel, Switzerland, in 1897. Its ultimate goal was to create a Jewish state in the Ottoman province of Palestine. In 1917, the Balfour Declaration gave British support to the creation of a Jewish homeland in this region.

In 1948, Israeli forces defeated five Arab armies to win independence for the Jewish state. Some 750,000 Palestinians fled the country. In 1956, Israel defeated Egypt, the most powerful nation in the Arab world, and gained control of the Sinai Peninsula. In 1967, Israel again defeated its Arab neighbors in the Six-Day War. In 1973, Israel defeated Arab armies that attacked on Yom Kippur, the Day of Atonement, the holiest day of the Jewish year.

These military losses greatly discredited the secular governments of the Arab world. A religious revival soon ensued as many Muslims came to believe that Allah was punishing them for their disobedience to *Shari'a*.

In addition to the renewed fervor that fueled radical Muslim movements, the Arab conflict with Israel also positioned America and the West as enemies of Islam. Radical Muslims view the Jews as traitors to God and adversaries of Islam. They believe Israel's continued occupation of "Palestine" to be an attack not only on the Palestinian people but on all Islam. As we noted with the Crusades, Muslims view the *Ummah* as the community of Muslims spanning all time and geography. An assault on one Muslim is aggression against all Islam.

America's continued support for Israel makes us complicit in this perceived attack on the Muslim world. Here is bin Laden's allegation:

> Palestine . . . has sunk under military occupation for more than 80 years. The British handed over Palestine, with your help and support, to the Jews, who have occupied it for more than 50 years; years overflowing with oppression, tyranny, crimes, killing, expulsion, destruction and devastation. The creation and continuance of Israel is one of the greatest crimes, and you are the leaders of its criminals. And of course there is no need to explain and prove the degree of American support for Israel. The creation of Israel is a crime which must be erased. Each and every person whose hands have become polluted in the contribution toward this crime must pay its price, and pay for it heavily.[8]

So long as America supports Israel in any way, radical Muslims will claim that we are the enemies of Islam and that they must attack us to defend their faith and people.

Conclusion

These four allegations explain radical Muslims' continued animosity toward America and the West. If you were the president of the United States, how would you meet the conditions for peace set out by our enemies?

You would need to withdraw support entirely from every Muslim government on earth, since none governs solely by *Shari'a*. Imagine the economic and military consequences of such a decision. You would need to cease all export of American culture to the Muslim world or reform our culture to conform to *Shari'a*. Imagine the technological and financial results of such an attempt.

You would need to apologize for the Crusades and every Western incursion into the Muslim world since, and withdraw all troops immediately from the Middle East and any Muslim nation. Imagine the global consequences of such an action. And you would need to end all support for Israel, the only democracy in the Middle East and our best friend in the region. Imagine the consequences for Israel and for the larger world.

Anything short of these actions will continue to provoke radical Muslims into attacks on our country and the Western world. This is a war unlike any we have fought. Killing bin Laden did not bring an end to al-Qaeda; destroying al-Qaeda would not bring an end to radical Islam.

As we will see in chapter 8, there are millions of Muslims around the world who agree with the accusations of our enemies. How have these claims become so persuasive for so many? For answers, we turn next to the most important scholar in the history of radical Islam.

ENDNOTES

1.   Sources for this section include Karen Armstrong, *The Battle for God: A History of Fundamentalism* (New York: Random House, 2000); Daniel Benjamin and Steven Simon, *The Age of Sacred Terror: Radical Islam's War Against America* (New York: Random House, 2003); John L. Esposito, *Unholy War: Terror In the Name of Islam* (New York: Oxford University Press, 2003); Bernard Lewis, *The Crisis of Islam: Holy War and Unholy Terror* (New York: Random House, 2004); Abraham Sarker, *Understand My Muslim People* (Newberg, Oregon: Barclay Press, 2004); and Lawrence Wright, *The Looming Tower: Al-Qaeda and the Road to 9/11* (New York: Vintage Books, 2007).

2.   http://www.guardian.co.uk/world/2002/nov/24/theobserver, accessed 16 July 2011.

3.   Lewis 4.

4.   John Esposito, noted scholar of Islam, states, "Perhaps no medieval scholar-activist has had more influence on radical Islamic ideology than Ibn Taymiyya" (45).

5.   Ibid., xx.

6.   http://www.guardian.co.uk/world/2002/nov/24/theobserver, accessed 16 July 2011.

7.   http://www.mideastweb.org/osamabinladen2.htm, accessed 17 July 2011.

8.   Ibid.

CHAPTER SIX

WHO WAS SAYYID QUTB? THE MIND BEHIND 9/11

Mankind today is on the brink of a precipice, not because of the danger of complete annihilation which is hanging over its head—this being just a symptom and not the real disease—but because humanity is devoid of those vital values which are necessary not only for its healthy development but also for its real progress. Even the Western world realizes that Western civilization is unable to present any healthy values for the guidance of mankind. It knows that it does not possess anything which will satisfy its own conscience and justify its existence. [1]

With these words, Sayyid Qutb[2] begins *Milestones*, the most significant single treatise in the history of radical Islam.[3] Qutb (1906-66) is regarded as "the father of modern fundamentalism," the figure who most influenced Usama bin Laden,[4] and "the greatest ideological influence on the contemporary Islamist movement."[5] *The New York Times* calls him "the father of the modern anti-Western jihadist movement in Islam."[6]

John Esposito, a prominent scholar on the Middle East, states, "It would be difficult to overestimate the role played by Sayyid Qutb in the reassertion of militant jihad. He was a godfather to Muslim extremist movements around the globe."[7] According to Ayman al-Zawahiri, the current leader of al-Qaeda,

> Sayyid Qutb's call for loyalty to God's oneness and to acknowledge God's sole authority and sovereignty was the spark that ignited the Islamic revolution against the enemies of Islam at home and abroad. The bloody chapters of this revolution continue to unfold day after day. The ideology of this revolution and the clarity of its course are getting firmer every day . . . until God Almighty inherits the earth and those who live on it."[8]

To understand why radical Muslims hate us, it is essential that we understand the revolutionary credo of Sayyid Qutb, the mind behind 9/11.

Early life

Qutb was born October 8, 1906, in a small village in Upper Egypt named Mush, a slum area along the Nile River. Raised by deeply religious parents, he was the oldest of five children. His intellectual gifts were apparent early—he had memorized the Qur'an by the age of 10.

He was educated at Dar al-'Ulum, a secular secondary college where Muslim Brotherhood founder Hasan al-Banna was also a student. After working as a literary critic, novelist, and school inspector for the Egyptian ministry of education, he was sent to the United States in 1948 to improve his English and study the American educational system. At the time he was Western in many ways, such as his dress and his love of Hollywood movies and classical music. He read the works of Darwin, Einstein, Byron, and Shelley, and especially enjoyed French literature.

Qutb visited New York City and studied at Wilson's Teachers College in Washington, D.C. (now the University of the District of Columbia). He then moved to Greeley, Colorado, where he earned an M.A. in education at Colorado State Teachers College (now the University of Northern Colorado).

Rejecting America

On his voyage to the States, Qutb met a drunken American woman who attempted to seduce him. His horror at Western immorality only increased as he encountered the postwar materialism and moral relativism of American culture. Ironically, Greeley was a very conservative town, a planned community that had made alcohol illegal. But Qutb saw in its green laws and resistance toward outsiders the kind of materialism and bigotry that he believed were characteristic of all Western culture.

He wrote about his experiences in *The America I Have Seen*. Much of his treatment of American history and culture was simply wrong. For instance, he claimed that we were still at war with Indians in 1949 and that American colonists pushed Latinos south toward Central America, though the colonists had not yet migrated west of the Mississippi River. He also claimed that the American divorce rate in 1950 was 40 percent when it was actually 3 percent.

He denounced jazz music as primitive and American sexual mores as scandalous. Even a church social he attended sparked his ire as he found its dance to be sexually suggestive. In his mind, America's fixation with athletics was further evidence of our primitive nature.

A "reborn" revolutionary

When he returned to Egypt on August 20, 1950, Qutb soon pronounced himself "reborn."[9] Here is his most significant autobiographical statement in *Milestones*:

> The person who is writing these lines has spent forty years of his life in reading books and in research in almost all aspects of human knowledge. He specialized in some branches of knowledge and he studied others due to personal interest. Then he turned to the fountainhead of his faith. He came to feel that whatever he had read so far was as nothing in comparison to what he found here. He does not regret spending forty years of his life in the pursuit of these sciences, because he came to know the nature of *Jahiliyyah*, its deviations, its errors and its ignorance, as well as its pomp and noise, its arrogant and boastful claims. Finally, he was convinced that a Muslim cannot combine these two sources—the source of Divine guidance and the source of *Jahiliyyah*—for his education (pp. 112-3).

Qutb soon joined the Muslim Brotherhood in its quest to remake Egypt in a fundamentalist Islamic mold. By 1952 he had become head of the Brotherhood's propaganda department and is still considered the only systematic thinker the movement has produced. An incredibly prolific author, he published more than 40 books, many of which were translated into English and Farsi and are still widely read across the Muslim world. While in prison Qutb also completed a 30-volume commentary on Islam's holy book called *In the Shadow of the Qur'an*.

His study of the Qur'an, along with his experiences in the West and at home in Egypt, hardened in him a resolve to overthrow all authorities except those who submit unconditionally to *Shari'a*. For these views he was arrested in 1954 and spent 10 years in prison. A year after his release he was arrested again after members of the Brotherhood attempted to assassinate Egyptian President Gamal Abd'el Nasser. He was tortured repeatedly by prison guards before being hanged on August 29, 1966.

Qutb laid out the path to Islamic revolution in his most influential work, *Malim if al-Tariq,* (*Milestones* or *Signposts on the Road*), written during his various imprisonments and published the year before his death. Its call to arms against the authorities was a significant reason for his second arrest and subsequent execution. His followers consider him a martyr to the cause of Islam.

"Qutb" in Arabic means "pole star," the pivot around which all else turns. The continued popularity and influence of his writings demonstrate the appropriateness of his name for radical Muslims the world over. His books are staples in Middle Eastern bookshops; *Milestones* has been called "one of the most influential works in Arabic of the last half century."[10]

Submitting to the sovereignty of God

Qutb's thesis is simple: Muslims must return to living only by the Qur'an and the *Hadith* and work until the world is governed by *Shari'a*.[11] His argument is extremely logical and can be summarized as a syllogism:

- ◆ Major premise: every person in the world must submit to the sovereignty of God, since there is no God but God and Muhammad is his prophet.
- ◆ Minor premise: any society governed according to principles not found in *Shari'a* defies the sovereignty of God.
- ◆ Conclusion: all such nations must be reformed until the world lives under the sovereignty of God as expressed in *Shari'a*.

This call to submit to divine sovereignty has always been God's call to humanity, as the entire universe exists under his authority (pp. 45-6). To develop a separate system from the one God has revealed is to cut ourselves off from our Creator (p. 46), an assertion the Qur'an makes clear: "Verily, this is My Way, leading straight: follow it: follow not (other) paths: they will scatter you about from His (great) Path: thus doth He command you, that ye may be righteous" (6:153).

God spent the first phase of Islamic history teaching his sovereignty and its implications to Muhammad in Mecca (pp. 23-4). The Prophet learned to reject the authority of all others, including priests, tribal leaders, wealthy people, and rulers (p. 24). He taught that people should seek and live by God's injunctions alone (p. 47), since the Muslim creed, "though concise, included the whole of life" (p. 48).

Just as God's natural laws govern the natural universe, so his moral laws govern the moral universe (pp. 88-9). All people are accountable to these laws (p. 90). Living by God's revealed laws is the best way to live on earth while preparing for heaven (p. 91).

Qutb's logic is compelling: Just as the Creator of the universe is the only One who has the right and ability to make its natural laws, so the Creator of humanity is the only One who has the right and ability to make its moral laws. We must live by God's natural and moral laws if we would live in harmony with him and his world. As a result, all people must live by *Shari'a* (pp. 107-8). This is the only way to serve God and live effectively in his world. Consequently we must refuse all other ways of life: "A Muslim has no relatives except those who share the belief in God" (p. 119).

Calling the world to true Islam: the "milestones"

Tragically, true Islam "vanished at the moment the laws of God became suspended on earth" (p. 9) with the abolishment of the caliphate on March 3, 1924. The Muslim world's rejection of *Sharia* explains its cultural decline in recent centuries (pp. 111-2). Now Islam must be restored to its original form, for only then can the Muslim community "fulfill its obligation as the leader of the world" (p. 10).

As a means to this end, it is necessary to "initiate the movement of Islamic revival in some Muslim country" (p. 11). Qutb's book sets out the "milestones" by which this movement can be initiated and led to success.

His pathway follows Muhammad's work, which unfolded in three stages: first, leading people to Islam through preaching (the Meccan period); second, defending Islam against its enemies (the early Medinian period); and third, fighting to advance Islam across the Arabian Peninsula (the later Medinian period).

According to Qutb, the same three stages should be followed today. The first stage is for Muslims to submit personally to the sovereignty of God. The second is for these Muslims to work against non-Muslim elements in their society. The third is for this group to gain "practical control of society" so that "every aspect of life should be under the sovereignty of God" (p. 35). Only when such an Islamic society has been created can non-Muslims living within it have a true opportunity to become Muslims (pp. 53-7).

Rejecting *Jahiliyyah*—the non-Muslim world

In Islamic history, *Jahiliyyah* has been used to describe the ignorance of the Arab people before Muhammad received his first revelation. Qutb accepts ibn Taymiyya's redefinition of the term, referring to the contemporary non-Muslim world as *Jahiliyyah*, which he defines as "ignorance of the divine guidance" (p. 11). He accuses all non-Muslim societies of joining in this global "rebellion against God's sovereignty on earth" (p. 11). Said differently, "*Jahiliyyah* is the worship of some people by others; that is to say, some people become dominant and make laws for others, regardless of whether these laws are against God's injunctions" (p. 130).

True Muslims must reject *Jahiliyyah*, for "either Islam will remain, or *Jahiliyyah*. . . . If it is not the truth, then it must be falsehood" (p. 130). In fact, "the foremost duty of Islam in this world is to depose *Jahiliyyah* from the leadership of man" (p. 131). This is because "*Jahiliyyah* is evil and corrupt, whether it be of the ancient or modern variety" (p. 132). *Jahili* influences are "backward" (p. 94) and must be refused, as "a slight influence from them can pollute the clear spring of Islam" (p. 116). Even family members must be rejected "if they openly declare their alliance with the enemies of Islam" (p. 119).

All other ways of life but Islam must be rejected: communism, because it replaces God's sovereignty with oppression of his creatures; capitalism, because it replaces divine sovereignty with greed and imperialism (p. 11); democracy, because it has become "infertile"; and Marxism, because it conflicts with human nature and has no future (p. 7).

In short, "the period of the Western system has come to an end" (p. 8). As a result, we need "a way of life which is harmonious with human nature, which is positive and constructive, and which is practicable. Islam is the only system which possesses these values and this way of life" (p. 8).

Unfortunately, *Jahiliyyah* opposes Islam in every way—it "crushes all elements which seem to be dangerous to its personality" (p. 46) since the aim of *jahili* society is "to block Islam" (p. 47). Muslims must refuse to compromise with *jahili* society in any way (p. 21). Instead, their "foremost objective is to change the practices of this society" (p. 21). Qutb wanted Muslims to "abolish the existing system and to replace it with a new system which in its character, principles and all its general and particular aspects, is different from the controlling *jahili* system" (pp. 46-7).

Exposing the immorality of the West

Qutb was especially incensed at the decadence he found when visiting America. Such immorality is basic to *Jahiliyyah*, so that "fornication" is common "among all *jahili* societies, old or new" (p. 28). While humanity has "drowned under the vast ocean of corruption" (p. 37), morality can be found only in Islam (p. 29).

Qutb documents his assertion by reference to the earliest period of Islam, "a zenith of perfection which had never been attained before and which cannot be attained afterwards except through Islam" (p. 30). He claims that this society was "an open and all-inclusive community in which people of various races, nations, languages and colors were members" (p. 49). In his view, these efforts "gave rise to a high level of civilization in a very short span of time, dazzling the whole world" (p. 49). Such a society was "never achieved by any other group of people in the entire history of mankind!" (p. 50).

By contrast, Western society is "drowning in lusts, steeped in low passions, rolling in filth and dirt" (p. 145). It is "backward" in its approach to family and the role of women:

> If woman's role is merely to be attractive, sexy and flirtatious, and if woman is freed from her basic responsibility of bringing up children; and if, on her own or under social demand, she prefers to become a hostess or a stewardess in a hotel or ship or air company, thus spending her ability for material productivity rather than in the training of human beings, because material production is considered to be more important, more valuable and more honorable than the development of human character, then such a civilization is "backward" from the human point of view, or *jahili* in the Islamic terminology (p. 98).

Qutb continues his critique of Western culture:

> Among *jahili* societies, writers, journalists and editors
> advise both married and unmarried people that free sexual
> relationships are not immoral. However, it is immoral if a
> boy uses his partner, or a girl uses her partner, for sex,
> while feeling no love in his or her heart. It is bad if a wife
> continues to guard her chastity while her love for her
> husband has vanished; it is admirable if she finds another
> lover. Dozens of stories are written about this theme; many
> newspaper editorials, articles, cartoons, serious and light
> columns all invite to this way of life. From the point of
> view of "human" progress, all such societies are not civi-
> lized but backward (p. 99).

He calls to the West:

> Look at these concepts of the Trinity, Original Sin, Sac-
> rifice and Redemption, which are agreeable neither to
> reason nor to conscience. Look at this capitalism with its
> monopolies, its usury and whatever else is unjust in it; at
> this individual freedom, devoid of human sympathy and
> responsibility for relatives except under the force of law;
> at this materialistic attitude which deadens the spirit; at
> this behavior, like animals, which you call "Free mixing of
> the sexes"; at this vulgarity which you call "emancipation
> of women," at these unfair and cumbersome laws of mar-
> riage and divorce, which are contrary to the demands of
> practical life; and at Islam, with its logic, beauty, humanity
> and happiness, which reaches the horizons to which man

strives but does not reach. It is a practical way of life and its solutions are based on the foundation of the wholesome nature of man (139).

Rejecting democracy

The central creed of Islam, which asserts the sovereignty of God alone, constitutes "a declaration of war against that authority which legislates laws not permitted by God" (25). Qutb's logic is clear: if God is the only sovereign, no laws are legitimate except his. Laws made by humanity must therefore be rejected in favor of the laws of God (p. 33).

Democratic governments rely on legislation, police, military, propaganda and the press, but they still cannot keep their citizens from "illegal and forbidden things" (p. 33). Qutb cites the United States' failure to prohibit alcohol as one example of the failure of democracy (p. 33).

Such a system "deifies human beings by designating others than God as lords over men" (p. 58). It establishes human assemblies with absolute power to legislate, "usurping the right which belongs to God alone" (p. 82).

By contrast, "*Shari'a* is best since it comes from God; the laws of His creatures can hardly be compared to the laws given by the Creator" (p. 36). Every other system has failed, from the Roman Empire to the British Empire and communism (pp. 50-1). As a result, "one should accept the *Shari'a* without any question and reject all other laws in any shape or form. This is Islam. There is no other meaning of Islam" (p. 36).

Waging *jihad* against non-Muslims

In seeking to abolish all *jahili* influences and establish a true *Shari'a*-based society, Muslims must combat the non-Muslim world in any way necessary. Qutb repudiates those who assert that *jihad* is to be waged only in defense of Islam, calling them "naïve" (p. 63) and "a product of the sorry state of the present Muslim generation" (p. 56). To the contrary, "no political system or material power should put hindrances in the way of preaching Islam" (p. 57). If someone does, "it is the duty of Islam to fight him until either he is killed or until he declares his submission" (p. 57).

In Muhammad's Meccan period he worked through persuasion until the message of Islam was established in the hearts of his followers. In his Medinian period he waged war to defend Islam and then to expand the Muslim movement. Today "only the final stages of the movement of *jihad* are to be followed; the initial or middle stages are not applicable" (p. 63). This "struggle is imposed upon Islam" so that "Islam has no choice but to defend itself against aggression" (p. 73). As "all the societies existing in the world today are *jahili*" (p. 80), all must be opposed.

Islam must confront all nations whether they are at war with it or not until they "submit to its authority by paying *jizyah*, which will be a guarantee that they have opened their doors for the preaching of Islam and will not put any obstacle in its way through the power of the state" (p. 73). The West must especially be opposed since its "crusading spirit" still motivates its relations with the Muslim world (p. 160).

Rejecting current Muslim societies

A group of people is truly Islamic only when "such a group has agreed to base its entire life on Islam and to obey God in all aspects of life" (p. 35). By contrast, "people are not Muslims, as they proclaim to be, as long as they live the life of *Jahiliyyah*" (p. 137). In fact, "anyone who serves someone other than God in this sense is outside God's religion, although he may claim to profess this religion" (p. 60). The task is "to return these ignorant people to Islam and make them into Muslims all over again" (p. 137).

Since all existing Muslim societies "have relegated the legislative attribute of God to others and submit to this authority" (p. 82), Muslims must "strike hard at all those political powers which force people to bow before them and which rule over them" (p. 61). True Muslims consider such societies "unIslamic and illegal" (p. 84), composed of "unbelievers" (p. 86).

Qutb rejects any version of Islam but his own:

> The Islamic society is not one in which people call themselves "Muslims" but in which the Islamic law has no status, even though prayer, fasting and *Hajj* are regularly observed; and the Islamic society is not one in which people invest their own version of Islam, other than what God and His Messenger—peace be on him—have prescribed and explained, and call it, for example, "progressive Islam" (p. 93).

In his view, moderate Muslims are not true Muslims. The difficult state of the Muslim world today is due to its rejection of true Islam: "The people in these countries have reached this wretched state by abandoning Islam, and not because they are Muslims" (p. 136).

In Qutb's view, any system but *Shari'a* is not Islamic, even if it exists in a democratic Muslim nation such as Turkey and Jordan. Autocratic leaders in countries such as Egypt and Saudi Arabia are likewise non-Muslim and must be overthrown.

Inviting people to true Islam

It is important to understand that Qutb's call to *jihad* is not a credo that seeks to gain lands or treasure from others. Unlike traditional wars that have been fought for geography and wealth, when someone accepts true Islam "we turn back and give his country back to him" (p. 71).

For example, the first Muslims forsook Mecca to build their *Ummah*, showing that land is secondary to Islam in importance (p. 123). While the

Arabian Peninsula was the "homeland of Islam" (p. 72), "a Muslim has no country except that part of the earth where the *Shari'a* of God is established and human relationships are based on the foundation of relationship with God; a Muslim has no nationality except his belief, which makes him a member of the Muslim community" (pp. 118-9).

Rather than fighting for land, true Islam fights for souls. Once a genuine Muslim nation has been created, those who live in it will have opportunity to choose to become Muslims themselves. Until this time, they could not live by *Shari'a* and thus could not choose true Islam.

In such a society, non-Muslims would be free to choose their religion (pp. 55-6). In this way Qutb reconciles Qur'an 2:256, "Let there be no compulsion in religion," with his call to "annihilate all those political and military powers which stand between people and Islam" (p. 57).

He explains that Islam is more than mere beliefs, striving "from the beginning to abolish all those systems and governments which are based on the rule of man over men and the servitude of one human being to another" (p. 61). As a result, it must construct a system built on *Shari'a* alone. Within that society, "every individual is free, under the protection of this universal system, to adopt any belief he wishes to adopt" (p. 61). Muslims use force "only to remove these obstacles" to true Islam (p. 72).

As a result, Islam is innocent of the charge that it is "a violent movement which imposed its belief upon people by the sword" (p. 76). In fact, in dealing with non-Muslims individually, "Islam looked at them from a height, as this is its true position, and addressed them with extreme love and kindness, as this is its true temperament, and explained everything to them with complete clarity, without any ambiguity, as this is its method" (p. 134). Muslims are motivated to share Islam with others "because we love them and we wish them well, although they may torture us" (p. 138).

To restate Qutb's logic: people cannot freely choose Islam if true Islam is not available for them to choose. As a result, a nation must be built that is governed strictly by *Shari'a*, as this is the only true Islam. Those who live in this nation would then be free to choose Islam or not as they wish. If they reject Islam they would pay the *jizyah* (Qur'an 9:29) and would be free to live as non-Muslims. This tax would replace the *zakat*—alms that are obligatory for Muslims—and would compensate for their exemption from military service.

Returning Muslims to true Islam

Qutb's objective is to return Islam to the purity of its first generation, an era that was "without comparison in the history of Islam, even in the entire history of man" (p. 15). Those living in this early period of Islamic history took their guidance only from the Qur'an and the model of the Prophet, a model Muslims should follow today (pp. 16-17).

This first generation of Muslims memorized the Qur'an 10 verses at a time and then acted on its teachings (p. 18). Those who chose to make Islam their way of life immediately cut themselves off from *Jahiliyyah* (p. 19), urged by monotheism to reject all authorities except God alone (p. 20).

In the same way,

> We should remove ourselves from all the influences of the *Jahiliyyah* in which we live and from which we derive benefits. We must return to that pure source from which those people derived their guidance, the source which is free from any mixing or pollution. We must return to it to derive from it our concepts of the nature of the universe, the nature of human existence, and the relationship of these two with the Perfect, the Real Being, God Most High. From it we must also derive our concepts of life, our principles of government, politics, economics and all other aspects of life (pp. 20-1).

Qutb's ultimate goal is a global *Ummah*, "a new social, economic and political system, in which the concept of the freedom of man is applied in practice" (p. 61). In his view, "This is God's religion and it is for the whole world" (p. 75). It is "the way of life ordained by God for all mankind" (p. 76). In this way "mankind can be dignified, today or tomorrow, by striving toward this noble civilization, by pulling itself out of the abyss of *Jahiliyyah* into which it is falling" (p. 103).

If this work requires martyrdom, so be it:

> All men die, and of various causes; but not all gain such victory, nor reach such heights, nor taste such freedom, nor soar to such limits of the horizon. It is God's choosing, and honoring a group of people who share death with the rest of mankind but who are singled out from other people for honor—honor among the noblest angels, nay, even among all mankind, if we measure them by the standards of the total history of generations of men (151).

Legacy

Sayyid Qutb's *Milestones* is required reading in radical Muslim circles the world over. It is considered by extremists to be as important to their movement as Vladimir Lenin's *What Is to Be Done?* was to communism. His ideas have sparked "Qutbism," a movement that seeks to promote his call to revolution.

We find Qutb's legacy foremost in America's ongoing conflict with al-Qaeda and Islamic terrorism. Professor Ibrahim Abu-Rabi, who teaches Islamic Studies and Christian-Muslim relations at Hartford Seminary in Hartford, Connecticut, calls Qutb "one of the most significant thinkers in modern and contemporary Arab Islamic resurgence" and states that he had a "major impact" on Usama bin Laden and Ayman al-Zawahiri.[12]

Qutb's brother, Muhammad (1919-present), was a teacher and mentor to the young Usama bin Laden at King Abdulaziz University in Jeddah, where bin Laden often attended his weekly public lectures. Muhammad edited and published his brother's books and made them the basis for the lectures that bin Laden heard. Sayyid was the third-grade Arabic teacher of Mahfouz Azzam, the uncle of Ayman al-Zawahiri; Qutb's writings greatly influenced the brilliant Egyptian physician's path into radicalism and al-Qaeda.

The leader of Al-Qaeda on the Arabian Peninsula, Anwar al-Awlaki, has also described his deep gratitude for Qutb's ideas. As we saw in chapter 5, Al-Awlaki has been tied to Major Nidal Hasan, the Fort Hood shooter, as well as the "Underwear Bomber" and the Times Square plot.[13] He speaks of reading "between 100 and 150 pages a day" of Qutb's writings and states, "I would be so immersed with the author I would feel Sayyid was with me in my cell speaking to me directly."[14]

Qutb's influence remains significant throughout the larger Muslim world as well.[15] His writings were influential for the founder of Hamas, the anti-Israeli party that rules the Gaza area today. Islamic Jihad, one of the most important Palestinian radical Islamist groups, relies on his endorsement of suicide bombers in justifying the strategy. The Sudanese Armed Islamic Movement, which has plotted assassinations, bombings, and training for terrorists, was heavily influenced by his worldview.

Qutb's influence is strong in South Asia and Southeast Asia, especially in Indonesia, where a large Muslim party called *al-Ikhwan* claims more than 2 million followers and bases its ideology primarily on Qutb's ideas. His ideas were so important to the Iranian revolution that his picture was placed on an Iranian stamp.

His writings have helped spark anti-Western sentiment in Tunisia and revolution in the Philippines and Algeria. And his legacy has been especially significant in his home country of Egypt. *Jama'at al-Jihad* ("Society of Struggle"), the group that assassinated Anwar el-Sadat in 1981, based its ideology on *Milestones*. On February 8, 2010, Egyptian President Hosni Mubarak arrested three Muslim Brotherhood members on the accusation that they belonged to a sect inspired by the thinking of Qutb. The men agreed that Qutb was the embodiment of the Islamist movement.

His ideas are influential among Muslims in the Western world as well. Professor Abu-Rabi's students find Qutb's works "very relevant in their Western environment"; the professor believes that Qutb exerts "a major impact on the minds of the young Muslims in Europe as well as the States." In summary, he was that man "whose lonely genius would unsettle Islam, threaten regimes across the Muslim world, and beckon to a generation of rootless young Arabs who were looking for meaning and purpose in their lives and would find it in jihad."[16]

Last, Qutb's affirmation of martyrdom as a glorious, blissful victory has been persuasive for suicide bombers. When Qutb received a death sentence from the Egyptian court, those present reported that a smile appeared on his face. In his endorsement of martyrdom for the cause of Islam he especially acts as "a model for modern Islamic radicalism."[17]

Conclusion

If a single book can be blamed for 9/11 and the War on Terror, that book is Sayyid Qutb's *Milestones*, the book that "ignited the radical Islamist movement."[18] Its call for anti-Western revolution and imposition of strict *Shari'a* on every nation is frightening. Its continued popularity around the world is even more so.

Professor John Zimmerman, whose research into Qutb's influence on 9/11 is the formative essay on the subject, concludes: "We may never know what the 19 Al-Qaeda hijackers of 11 September 2011 were thinking as they steered the airplanes toward the twin towers of the World Trade Center, the Pentagon and an open field in Pennsylvania. However, we can be certain that they were immersed in the ideas of Sayyid Qutb."

Now, in many *madrassas* around the world, a new generation of young Muslims is drinking deeply from the poisoned well of Qutb's radicalism. What acts of terror will they incite? How can we win the battle for their minds before it's too late? We turn next to a survey of questions concerning the future of radical Islam and to practical steps we can take in confronting this enemy. Finally, we will consider the spiritual implications of the War on Terror, for here we find the ultimate answers to America's greatest challenge.

ENDNOTES

1. Sayyid Qutb, *Milestones* (Damascus, Syria: Dar al-Ilm, n.d.) 7. For ease of documentation I will cite page numbers from this treatise in the body of the chapter rather than as endnotes.

2. As with other Arabic names transliterated into English, "Sayyid" can be spelled a variety of ways—"Sayyed," "Sayed," and "Seyyid" (the spelling on the English translation of *Milestones* I have used) are all found in print. I have followed the most common usage in spelling his first name as "Sayyid." I have also standardized his spelling of Arabic terms such as *jihad* to make them consistent with other usage in this book.

3. Sources for this chapter include: Daniel Benjamin and Steven Simon, *The Age of Sacred Terror: Radical Islam's War Against America* (New York: Random House, 2003); John Calvert, *Sayyid Qutb and the Origins of Radical Islamism* (New York: Columbia University Press, 2010), a definitive treatment of the subject; John L. Esposito, *Unholy War: Terror In the Name of Islam* (New York: Oxford University Press, 2002); Efraim Karsh, *Islamic Imperialism: A History,* updated edition [New Haven, Connecticut; Yale University Press, 2007; Luke Loboda, *The Thought of Sayyid Qutb: Radical Islam's Philosophical Foundations* (http://www.ashbrook.org/publicat/thesis/loboda/home.html), accessed 15 July 2011; Lawrence Wright, *The Looming Tower: Al-Qaeda and the Road to 9/11* (New York: Vintage Books, 2006); and John C. Zimmerman, "Sayyid Qutb's Influence on the 11 September Attacks," *Terrorism and Political Violence* 16:2, 222-52 (http://dx.doi.org/10.1080/09546550490480993, accessed 15 July 2011).

4. http://www.guardian.co.uk/world/2001/nov/01/afghanistan.terrorism3, accessed 15 July 2011.

5. Zimmerman, quoting French Arabist Gilles Kepel.

6. http://www.nytimes.com/2010/05/09/world/09awlaki.html?pagewanted=5&hp, accessed 15 July 2011.

7. Esposito 56.

8. Laura Mansfield, *His Own Words: Translation and Analysis of the Writings of Dr. Ayman al Zawahiri* (http://books.google.com/books?id=Mt5_aNiyqUoC&printsec=frontcover#v=onepage&q&f=false) accessed 17 July 2011.

9. Karsh calls Qutb "a born-again Muslim, breaking with his secular life style only in his forties" (214).

10. Benjamin and Simon 63. In summarizing the intellectual currents behind radical Islam they call Qutb "the source."

11. To avoid awkwardness, the descriptions that follow allow Qutb to state his assertions but do not imply endorsement of his ideology.

12. http://www.religioscope.com/info/dossiers/textislamism/qutb_aburabi.htm, accessed 15 July 2011.

13. http://theweek.com/article/index/102685/who-is-anwar-al-awlaki, accessed 15 July 2011.

14. http://www.nytimes.com/2010/05/09/world/09awlaki.html?pagewanted=5&hp, accessed 15 July 2011.

15. See Zimmerman for an extended discussion of this subject.

16. Wright 12.

17. Loboda.

18. Wright 213.

CHAPTER SEVEN

WHAT DOES THE FUTURE HOLD?
ISSUES FACING ISRAEL AND THE WEST

Most Americans believe the "War on Terror" began on September 11, 2001. In actuality, Islamic terrorists have been attacking and killing Americans for more than 30 years. We can trace the present war to the Islamic Revolution in Iran and its seizure of our embassy on November 4, 1979. The success of this offensive against our country emboldened Islamic terrorists.

Consider the atrocities committed against America by radical Muslims in the years since:

- On April 18, 1983, Hezbollah sent a suicide bomber to attack our embassy in Beirut, Lebanon, killing 63 employees and wounding 120.
- In October 23, 1983, another Hezbollah suicide bomber blew up an American barracks in the Beirut

airport, killing 241 U.S. Marines in their sleep and wounding 81.

- On September 20, 1984, the U.S. embassy annex near Beirut was hit by another truck bomb.
- On December 3, 1984, a Kuwaiti airliner was hijacked and two Americans murdered.
- On June 14, 1985, Hezbollah operatives hijacked TWA flight 847 and held it captive for two weeks.
- On October 7, 1985, a terror group hijacked the *Achille Lauro*, an Italian cruise ship, throwing a wheelchair-bound elderly American named Leon Klinghoffer overboard.
- On December 27, 1985, Libyan operatives bombed the Rome and Vienna airports, killing five Americans.
- On December 21, 1988, Libyan terrorists bombed Pan Am flight 103 over Lockerbie, Scotland, killing 270 people (190 were Americans).
- On February 26, 1993, a truck bomb exploded in the parking garage of the World Trade Center, killing six and wounding more than a thousand.
- On April 14, 1993, Iraqi operatives attempted to assassinate American President George H. W. Bush.
- On June 25, 1996, the Khobar Towers in Dhahran, Saudi Arabia were blasted by a truck bomb, killing 19 American soldiers and wounding 240 others.
- On August 7, 1998, car bombs killed more than 200 at our embassies in Kenya and Tanzania.
- On October 12, 2000, suicide bombers attacked the USS *Cole* in Yemen, killing 17 sailors and injuring 39.
- On September 11, 2001, 19 terrorists killed 2,819 Americans.[1]

What is the future of this conflict? In this chapter we'll address some of the questions that are critical to our ongoing engagement with radical Islam.[2]

Who are Sunnis and Shias?[3]

The 1979 Iranian hostage crisis brought the word *Shi'ite* to Western attention. It was the first time most Americans had heard the word. The crisis caused many to see the term as synonymous with radical Muslims, though each of the 9/11 terrorists was Sunni, the other main division in Islam. What are the differences?

A very brief description of the two groups begins with the successors of the Prophet Muhammad. His son-in-law, Ali, was the fourth *caliph*. Many of Ali's followers believed that he was the only rightful heir to the Prophet; they became known as *Shia* ("partisans" or "party of Ali").

Shias comprise 15 percent of the Muslim world and are the majority in Iran (where they make up 90-95 percent of the population), Iraq, Bahrain, and Azerbaijan. They form significant minorities in Lebanon and Yemen (where they are nearly half the population), Pakistan, India, Iraq, Turkey, Kuwait, Afghanistan, Syria, and Saudi Arabia. In parts of the Middle East where oil reserves are the richest—Iran, Iraq, and the Persian Gulf coast, including eastern Saudi Arabia—they are the majority.

"Sunnis" (from *sunna*, "habit" or "usual practice") comprise 85 percent of the Muslim world. They believe that the *caliphs* who followed Muhammad were the proper successors of the Prophet. Several interpretive schools have evolved within their tradition.[4]

Both groups have spawned radical Muslims—there is nothing unique to either that makes its followers more likely to become radicalized. However, there is a theology specific to some Shias that is especially significant for our discussion, as we will see next.

Is Mahmoud Ahmadinejad a threat?

In 1953, CIA forces deposed the democratically elected leader of Iran and restored the Western-aligned Shah as absolute monarch. The Ayatollah Ruhollah Khomeini led a revolt against the Shah on New Year's Day 1979 that deposed him and birthed the present Islamic Republic of Iran.

The current president of Iran is Mahmoud Ahmadinejad. In the view of many observers, he is the most dangerous Muslim on earth. The former mayor of Tehran, he was elected president in 2005 and reelected four years later in voting marred by widespread allegations of fraud. He has made world headlines by calling the Holocaust a "myth" and describing Israel as "filthy bacteria" and "the most criminal people in the world." He tells his people that "the United States and the Zionist regime are their main enemies" and promises that "this regime would soon be swept away."[5]

Waiting for the *Mahdi*

His theology is the reason Ahmadinejad is an especially troubling figure. Like the majority of Shias he is a "Twelver," following a doctrine that claims that the 12th *imam* after Muhammad will return at the end of history to dominate the world for Islam. (*Imam* is the title of Shia's supreme spiritual leader.) They believe that this *imam*, Abu al-Qasim Muhammad, was hidden by God in 872 and transported to a transcendent realm in 934 (this event is called the "occultation"). In their theology he is still alive and waiting to reappear at the end of history as the *Mahdi* ("the guided one"), a kind of Muslim Messiah. Many Shias voice and write prayers to him regularly.

Many Twelvers believe that a time of great chaos will precede the coming of the *Mahdi*. In the minds of some, Israel must be destroyed before the *Mahdi* will reappear. If this belief explains Ahmadinejad's quest for nuclear technology, the future of the Middle East and the world may be affected as a result.

On October 26, 2005, Ahmadinejad declared that Israel must be "wiped off the map."[6] The next year he stated that "the Zionist regime of Israel is like a rotten, dried tree that will be annihilated by one storm. Like it or not, the Zionist regime is headed toward annihilation."[7]

Developing nuclear technology

Shortly after he assumed Iran's presidency, Ahmadinejad revived the nation's long-dormant nuclear development program. In February 2010 Iran announced that it would begin enriching its stockpile of uranium. That same month, United Nations nuclear inspectors reported evidence that Iran had been working to develop a nuclear warhead. Some American officials believe that Tehran has obtained advanced missiles from North Korea that would enable it to strike at Western European capitals and Moscow.

The Stuxnex computer virus that emerged in July 2010 appears to have wiped out roughly a fifth of Iran's nuclear centrifuges, delaying its ability to produce its first nuclear arms. However, in June 2011 Iran announced it would triple its production of nuclear fuel. A month earlier, U.N. nuclear inspectors claimed to possess evidence that Tehran is working on a highly sophisticated nuclear triggering technology that could be used for only one purpose: to set off a nuclear weapon.

Documentary evidence also shows that Iran has conducted studies involving the removal of the conventional payload from the warhead of the Shahab-3 missile and replacing it with a nuclear payload. The Shahab-3, which stands 56 feet tall, has been used in parades draped with banners reading, "Wipe Israel off the map."[8]

Threatening Israel and the West

Many warn that Ahmadinejad's constant references to the destruction of Israel should be taken seriously. Israeli Prime Minister Benjamin Netanyahu is an example. Speaking to CNN's Piers Morgan on March 17, 2011, he reminded listeners that when he was first elected prime minister 15 years ago and spoke to a joint session of the U.S. Congress, he stated that "the single greatest threat facing the world and my own country was the arming of Iran with nuclear weapons." He told Morgan that Iran has "enriched enough material now almost for three nuclear bombs" and that "they're building long-range ICBMs" that would reach far beyond Israel.[9]

It's not hard to conclude that Mahmoud Ahmadinejad is pursuing nuclear development so he can create weapons that will hasten the coming of the *Mahdi*. Many Muslims claim that when the *Mahdi* appears he will protect Muslims and rule the world for Islam. If Ahmadinejad believes that launching a nuclear strike on Israel would bring the *Mahdi* and that this Messiah would protect Iran and the Muslim world from Israeli and American retribution, there would be no deterrent to such aggression. He could create another Holocaust in the time it takes a missile to fly from Tehran to Jerusalem. Now you can see why many consider Ahmadinejad to be so dangerous.

Is the "Arab Spring" a good thing?

In January 2011, who would have imagined that Egyptian president Hosni Mubarak would be displaced by a pro-democracy movement fueled by social media? Or that activists would oust the dictator of Tunisia, force the leader of Jordan to replace his government, and fill the streets of Tehran and Tripoli with demonstrators? How did this unprecedented uprising in the Arab world begin? What is its relevance to radical Islam?

How it happened

In 2005 a group in Egypt organized "Youth for Change," but many tried working through established parties without success. In 2008 the group attempted to organize isolated labor strikes, but bad weather and police crackdowns defeated their efforts. In 2010, their movement gained a strategic ally when Wael Ghonim, the now-famous Google marketing executive, joined their ranks.

He set up a Facebook group named for Khalid Said, the young Egyptian who was beaten to death by police last year. His page attracted hundreds of thousands of followers. They focused on January 25, which is Police Day in Egypt, a holiday that celebrates a police revolt suppressed by the British in 1952. More than 100,000 signed up to join their protest, and the rest is history.

Their movement illustrates the power of social media. Clay Shirky, an expert on social media, has documented numerous examples of social revolution fomented in this way.[10] In 2001, text messages produced a million-person crowd in Manila, forcing the removal of Philippine President Joseph Estrada. In 2004, demonstrations organized by text messaging led to the ouster of Spanish Prime Minister Jose Maria Aznar. In 2009, massive protests coordinated by social media caused the downfall of the Communist Party in Moldova. Later that year, the Green Movement in Iran made global headlines, fueled by social media. Now we can add the Egyptian revolt to the list.

Why it matters

Why is this movement relevant to the rest of the world?

Egypt is most populous nation in the Arab world and Israel's most significant political partner in the region. It supplies 40 percent of Israel's natural gas and controls the Suez Canal, through which oil shipments are carried from the Red Sea to the Mediterranean and on to Europe and America. No one knows what would happen to the price of gasoline if these shipments were disrupted or halted. A regime in this region sympathetic to al-Qaeda would strengthen radical Muslims around the world.

Is this movement toward democracy a positive development in the fight against radical Islam?

Journalist Melik Kaylan has chided America for refusing to encourage our values in Iraq.[11] During the Cold War, he argues, we offered the world a coherent Western way of life. Today we no longer believe we have anything to teach other cultures. It is conventional wisdom that there are no absolutes—so long as we're sincere in our beliefs and tolerant of others, we'll all get along.

Here's the problem: If we "liberate" a people so they can conduct democratic elections but do not help them develop tools of democracy such as political parties and a free press, we can leave them victim to whatever forces are most organized at the time. There will almost always be a militant opposition to the existing government ready to step into the power vacuum that results, usually to the detriment of the people.

Will this happen in Egypt and other Arab nations?

Is the Muslim Brotherhood a radical group?

This concern leads us to the Muslim Brotherhood (*Ikhwan al-Mus-limim*), an organization founded in 1928 by Hasan al-Banna. Considered "the mother of all Islamist movements,"[12] it was originally designed to Islamize society through promotion of Islamic morals, values, and law. It has combined social welfare, political activism, and religion. Its creed: "Allah is our objective. The Prophet is our leader. Qur'an is our law. Jihad is our way. Dying in the way of Allah is our highest hope."

Al-Banna, a 22-year-old elementary school teacher, led this Islamic revival movement after the Ottoman Empire collapsed following World

War I. He accused the Egyptian government of being passive with regard to Israel. After a member of the Brotherhood assassinated the Egyptian Prime Minister on December 28, 1948, the group was banned inside Egypt. It aligned with the military coup that ended British rule in 1952 but soon fell into conflict with President Gamal Abd'el Nasser and was banned again.

As we have seen, the Brotherhood produced Ayman al-Zawahiri, the eye surgeon who is now the leader of al-Qaeda. It also birthed Sayyid Qutb, the writer who inspired Usama bin Laden and radical Muslims around the world.

What are its intentions now? Some observers believe it has become a social organization committed to peaceful reform and the democratic process. Others believe that it is still committed to the restoration of the caliphate and the strict application of *Shari'a*.

What no one disputes is that the Brotherhood is the best-organized political movement in Egypt. If elections were held today, many observers believe that the group would gain a significant if not majority position in the new government. While the Brotherhood has promised to contest less than half the seats in the new parliament, skeptics worry that their proxies will run for the other seats in an attempt to control the new government.

What would happen then to Egypt's treaty with Israel and its agreement to supply energy to the Jewish state? What about control of the Suez Canal and oil shipments to the West that come through this channel every day? What role would a radical Muslim government in Egypt play in the larger Middle East?

What is the future for Hamas?

Israel is surrounded by potential enemies—the Muslim Brotherhood to the south, Hamas to the southwest, and Hezbollah to the north. Of the three, Hamas has been most difficult in recent years.

First, some background: The primary areas of Palestinian occupation in Israel are called the West Bank and the Gaza Strip. The former covers 2,177 square miles, an area slightly smaller than the state of Delaware. Its name is derived from its location on the western bank of the Jordan River and the Dead Sea; its population exceeds 2.5 million people. The latter is an area 25 miles long and 4 to 7.5 miles wide with a population of 1.6 million people.

The West Bank is governed by Fatah, an acronym for "Palestinian National Liberation Movement." This political party was founded in 1959 by Yasser Arafat, who led the group until his death in 2004.

The Gaza Strip is governed by Hamas ("fervor"), which is an acronym (spelled backwards) for "Islamic Resistance Movement." The group's origins go back to Sheikh Ahmed Yassin, who began his movement in the late 1960s as an offshoot of the Muslim Brotherhood. In 1973, he established the "Islamic Center" to coordinate the Brotherhood's activities in Gaza and founded Hamas as their political arm in 1987. It published its official charter in 1988, calling for the destruction of Israel and raising "the banner of Allah over every inch of Palestine."

For much of the group's history, the military wing of Hamas, called the *Izz al-Din al-Qassam Brigade,* has sponsored terrorism against Israel. It has repeatedly launched rocket attacks at Israeli towns and sponsored a series of suicide bombers before Israel constructed a security fence around its borders. The Brigade claims more than a thousand members and is believed to have killed more than 500 people.

Hamas has also engaged in social and political work, funding healthcare clinics, orphanages, sports leagues, mosques, and schools. More than 90 percent of its work is cultural, social, and educational.

The group operated as an opposition party in Gaza until winning parliamentary elections in 2006. Since that time it has been at odds with Fatah, which still governs the West Bank, so that the Palestinian people have had no unified government or advocate. The two parties have pledged cooperation and a mutual election in 2012. Whether Hamas will be a partner in peace negotiations with Israel remains to be seen.

Will Hezbollah attack Israel?

Hezbollah ("Party of God") was founded in 1982 in Lebanon by Sheikh Mohammed Hussein Fadlallah, heir to the former coalition of militant groups known as Islamic Jihad. Since its beginnings it has been sponsored by Iran and Syria.

Hassan Nasrallah is the group's senior political leader. Najib Miqati, recently elected as prime minister of Lebanon, was chosen by Hezbollah for this post. His election represents the first time the organization has been involved formally in the government of Lebanon.

The organization is a major provider of social services, hospitals, schools, and agricultural services for Shias living in Lebanon. Its militant wing has been defined by the United States as a terrorist organization.

The year after its founding, the group launched a truck bomb on the U.S. Marine barracks in Beirut, killing more than 200. In 1992 they bombed the Israeli embassy in Argentina, killing 29, and bombed a Jewish community center in 1994, killing 95. Periodic border skirmishes and shelling escalated into full-scale war with Israel in the summer of 2006. A United Nations-brokered peace ended the conflict, but tensions in the region remain high. When I was last in Israel, I met many officials who assume that another war with Lebanon is inevitable.

What is the future in Afghanistan?

In 1994, two teenage girls were kidnapped and raped by followers of a warlord in Afghanistan. A group of 30 students joined their village cleric, Mullah Muhammad Omar, in rescuing the girls and hanging the group's commander from a tank barrel. This is the most common explanation for the birth of the Taliban (literally "students").

The group grew in popularity and strength, eventually gaining the support of religious parties within neighboring Pakistan. In the chaos of post-Soviet Afghanistan, their enforcement of order and law was a welcome relief to the population. They conquered Kandahar, Afghanistan's second largest city, at the end of 1994 and captured the capital city of Kabul two years later. By 1998 they occupied 90 percent of the country.

Before long, it became clear that the Taliban would enforce a puritanical version of Islam akin to Wahhabism. The group provided sanctuary to Usama bin Laden and formed a crucial base for the rise of al-Qaeda.

After 9/11, when the Taliban refused to expel bin Laden and end its support for terrorism, a U.S.-led coalition invaded Afghanistan to remove them from power. Kabul fell on November 13, 2001. A new constitution was adopted on January 4, 2004, creating a parliamentary democracy. Hamid Karzai was elected president and reelected five years later. Charges of widespread corruption persist against his government.

U.S. forces remain in the country as the Afghan government develops a military force capable of preventing the return of al-Qaeda and other terrorist organizations. The United States has now been fighting in Afghanistan longer than any war in our nation's history. Whether our announced plan to withdraw all troops by 2014 will strengthen or harm Afghan security remains to be seen.

Is Turkey turning radical?

I have traveled often in Turkey over the years and have been amazed by the contrast between that nation and other Muslim countries. Women in Turkey are not required to wear Islamic clothing; men often wear Western suits. The government functions as a parliamentary democracy where clerics have no political office, unlike Iran, for instance, where Shi'ite Supreme Leader Khamenei is the de-facto leader of the nation.

However, in 2010 Turkish voters approved amendments to their national constitution which gave unprecedented powers to the current prime minister, Recep Tayyip Erdogan. Erdogan leads the Justice and Development Party, which advocates a much stronger Islamic character for the nation.

In May 2010, Erdogan engaged in negotiations with Iran over a nuclear fuel swap agreement. That same month, a flotilla launched from Turkey was intercepted by Israeli forces. The ensuing bloodshed was described by Erdogan as "inhuman state terror," while Israel claims that the flotilla was intended to bolster terrorism against its people.

Opposition leaders claim that the government's recent actions are part of a pattern designed to transform Turkey into an Islamic theocracy. Why does this issue matter to the West?

Turkey possesses the second largest military in NATO, after the United States; its economy is the largest in the Muslim world. It is plausible that the current trajectory could lead the nation to seek an elevated role in the Muslim world akin to the Ottoman Empire seven centuries ago.

Conclusion

America's wars in Iraq and Afghanistan will ultimately cost more than $3.2 trillion. Some 225,000 people have been killed, including 137,000 civilians. War refugees exceed 7.8 million, equivalent to the total populations of Connecticut and Kentucky fleeing their homes.[13] The issues we have discussed in this chapter could extend this conflict far into the future.

Imagine a Middle East with militant Islamic regimes bordering Israel in Egypt, Gaza, the West Bank, and Lebanon, each pledged to the Jewish state's destruction. Then imagine armies from Turkey or Iran aiding such aggression, the latter with nuclear arms. While none of these scenarios may come to pass in the near future, all of them could. Not to mention the fact that al-Qaeda and other terrorist organizations will undoubtedly continue their attacks on America and the West.

Is there a way to end our ongoing conflict with radical Muslims? We turn next to practical steps we can take in winning the War on Terror.

ENDNOTES

1. Norman Podhoretz, *World War IV: The Long Struggle Against Islamofascism* (New York: Doubleday, 2007) 28-36.

2. Sources for this section include Daniel Benjamin and Steven Simon, *The Age of Sacred Terror: Radical Islam's War Against America* (New York: Random House, 2003) and the Council on Foreign Relations website (www.cfr.org), whose articles on various groups involved with radical Islam are authoritative.

3. An excellent introduction to this subject is Lesley Hazleton, *After the Prophet: The Epic Story of the Shia-Sunni Split* (New York: Anchor Books, 2009).

4. The *Hanafi* are the oldest tradition, founded in Baghdad and comprising 30 percent of Sunni Muslims. They are concentrated in Turkey, Egypt, and the Indian subcontinent, and are most open to modern culture and ideas. The *Malaki* make up 25 percent of the Sunni Muslim world. They were founded in Mecca in the 8th century and are traditionally Arabic; they are especially dominant in North Africa. The *Shafi* originated in Baghdad. They are a liberalized form of *Malaki*, comprising 15 percent of Sunni Muslims worldwide and are predominant in Indonesia, Malaysia, and the Philippines. The *Hanbali* were founded in the mid-9th century, predominantly in the Arabian Peninsula. They are the strictest form of Sunni Islam and comprise less than 5 percent of Sunni Muslims worldwide (Sarker 72).

5. http://www.adl.org/main_International_Affairs/ahmadinejad_words.htm?Multi_page_sections=sHeading_1, accessed 16 July 2011.

6. http://www.nytimes.com/2005/10/26/world/africa/26iht-iran.html, accessed 16 July 2011.

7. http://www.pbs.org/newshour/bb/middle_east/jan-june06/iran_4-14.html, accessed 16 July 2011.

8. http://topics.nytimes.com/top/news/international/countriesandterritories/iran/nuclear_program/index.html, accessed 16 July 2011.

9. http://transcripts.cnn.com/TRANSCRIPTS/1103/17/pmt.01.html, accessed 16 July 2011.

10. http://www.foreignaffairs.com/articles/67038/clay-shirky/the-political-power-of-social-media, accessed 16 July 2011.

11. http://www.worldaffairsjournal.org/articles/2011-JanFeb/full-Kaylan-JF-2011.html, accessed 16 July 2011.

12. http://www.cfr.org/africa/egypts-muslim-brotherhood/p23991, accessed 16 July 2011.

13. http://costsofwar.org/, accessed 29 June 2011.

CHAPTER EIGHT

WHAT DO WE DO NOW?
SEVEN WAYS TO RESPOND TO RADICAL ISLAM

How many radical Muslims are there in the world?

Between 2001 and 2007, the Gallup organization conducted the most comprehensive survey of contemporary Muslims ever done. They analyzed a sample representing more than 90 percent of the world's Muslims, publishing their results in a fascinating study titled *Who Speaks for Islam? What A Billion Muslims Really Think.*[1]

The results of their study are frightening, encouraging, and enlightening.

The size of the problem

Gallup defined a "radical" Muslim as one who believes that the 9/11 attacks were "completely" justified and views the United States unfavorably. Their surveys revealed that only seven percent of the world's Muslims fit this description and refers to them as "radicalized."[2] When I first read that report several years ago I was relieved to learn that radical Muslims make up such a small percentage of the larger Muslim world. Then I did the math: seven percent of 1.6 billion people is 112 million people.

In World War II, Allied armies fought against a combined military of 28 million soldiers; during the Cold War we faced a Soviet army of some 13 million.[3] A global force of 112 million people who agree with Usama bin Laden that Americans are enemies of Islam who must be killed is a terrifying reality.

Now let's add this fact: half of radicalized Muslims the world over say that willingness to "sacrifice one's life for something one believes in" is "completely justifiable."[4] Here's a troubling question: Does this response indicate that half of the world's 112 million radical Muslims would be willing to serve their cause as suicide bombers? If Gallup's surveys overstate the case tenfold, we are still facing five million potential suicide attackers.

And the problem is even more serious than statistics suggest.

The complexity of the problem

Gallup's surveys do not reflect the motivation underlying this threat. Unlike the armies of Naziism or communism, these enemies are fighting a spiritual war. They will not be defeated by killing their leaders or capturing their soldiers and cities. They are convinced that they are fighting and dying for the only true God and that he will reward their sacrifice eternally.

Nor do Gallup's surveys reflect the strategic challenge radical Muslims pose, a threat all out of proportion to its numeric size. For example, the 19 terrorists who perpetrated 9/11 were able to kill more Americans than died at Pearl Harbor. Al-Qaeda has never employed more than a few hundred commanders around the world, yet we continue to commit hundreds of thousands of troops and billions of dollars to defeat them.

In this age of "microterrorism," a few people can cripple a city or an economy. Al-Qaeda's webzine *Inspire* recently described the organization's strategy: "We do not need to strike big. Attacking the enemy . . . is to bleed the enemy to death," a tactic they describe as "the strategy of a thousand cuts." Another essay boasts that the cargo plane attack in October 2010 cost the organization two phones, two printers, and shipping costs, for a total of $4,200.[5]

And Gallup's numbers do not reflect the escalating concentration of radical Muslims in places like Yemen, Iraq, and North Africa or the growing problem of radicalization in America and Europe, where there are jihadist organizations in every country west of the former Iron Curtain except Ireland.[6] Ours is indeed "the age of sacred terror."[7] How should Western nations respond to the greatest threat we've ever faced?

Step one: Know the enemy

"Know your enemy and know yourself and you can fight a hundred battles without disaster," advised Chinese general Sun Tzu. The first step Americans should take in confronting radical Islam is knowing radical Muslims.

Most people in the West picture radical Muslims as backwards, uneducated, and impoverished. Gallup's studies proved the opposite to be true. Radicalized Muslims are on average more educated than moderates—67 percent have secondary or higher educations, compared with 52 percent of moderates. Almost half supervise others at work; 64 percent believe their standard of living is improving, compared with 55 percent of moderates.[8]

Al-Qaeda's leader is an example. Dr. Ayman al-Zawahiri was one of the most prominent eye surgeons in Egypt before turning to radicalism. His father was a professor of pharmacology; his brother was a highly respected physician. A 1995 obituary in a Cairo newspaper for a family member mentioned 46 members of al-Zawahiri's extended family, 31 of whom were doctors, chemists, or pharmacists. Among the others were an ambassador, a judge, and a member of parliament. Ayman and his twin sister, Umnya, were both at the top of their classes all through medical school. Ayman's classmates considered him a genius.[9]

Radical Islam's leaders are not ignorant people. Most come from middle-class or upper-class backgrounds. They view themselves as protectors and defenders of Islam, willing to make any sacrifice for their faith. We underestimate them if we see them differently.

Step two: Define the problem

Remember the two tenets of radical Islam as expressed by Usama bin Laden and others: (1) the West has been attacking the Muslim world since the Crusades, so that *jihadists* are defending Islam by attacking us; (2) citizens in the democratic West support their leaders and military, making them combatants and enemies of Islam.

As we have seen, these tenets are expressed in four accusations against America and the Western world:

- We impose non-Muslim governments on the Muslim world.
- We impose non-Muslim values on Muslim culture.
- We are "Crusaders" who seek to conquer their lands and people.
- We support the "Zionists" in their aggression against Palestinians and Islam.

Gallup's research substantiates these convictions among radical Muslims around the world. By far the leading motivation for their hatred of the West is our perceived aggression against their nations.[10] This sense of victimization and oppression is common to "fundamentalist" movements,[11] but is especially obvious among radical Muslims.

For instance, there had never been a suicide attack in Iraq before troops from the United States arrived. Two-thirds of al-Qaeda suicide terrorists from 1995 to 2004 were from countries where the United States has maintained a heavy military presence since 1990.[12]

We intend our military presence in the Middle East to be a force for peace and stability, but radical Muslims are convinced that we have invaded their most sacred lands. Saudi Arabia is home to Mecca and Medina, their two holiest cities. They believe we came to the Kingdom in 1991 not to defend it but to occupy it. Iraq and its capital, Baghdad, was the seat of the caliphate for half a millennium. In their minds we came not to remove a brutal dictator but to become one.

As a result, radical Muslims are convinced that our presence in the Muslim world is not intended to foster democracy and that we will not allow Muslims to fashion their own political future. They also cite our immoral culture as a top reason for resentment of the West.[13]

John Esposito concludes his insightful analysis of radical Islam with this assertion:

> While some forms of terrorism, like some forms of cancer, respond to radical surgery, this deadly disease can only be effectively countered first by understanding how it originates, grows stronger, and spreads and then by taking action. The cancer of global terrorism will continue to afflict the international body until we address its political and economic causes, causes that will otherwise continue to provide a breeding ground for hatred and radicalism, the rise of extremist movements, and recruits for the bin Ladens of the world.[14]

Step three: Encourage democracy

Surprisingly, a significantly higher percentage of radical Muslims (50 percent vs. 35 percent of moderates) say that "moving toward greater governmental democracy" will advance progress in the Arab/Muslim world.[15] Since America's military presence in the Middle East is the single greatest catalyst fueling radical Islam, we must act decisively to counteract the allegation that we are invading "Crusaders" rather than agents of democratic reform.

What do Muslims want?

To do so, we must first reject the assertion that Islam and democracy are incompatible. For radical Islamists such as Sayyid Qutb, any system of laws not based solely on *Shari'a* must be rejected. It is true that only one in four Muslim-majority countries is led by democratically elected governments. However, we must remember that most of these populations were subjected to colonial rule for centuries; many of their nations were created after World War II and are only decades old.[16]

When asked their political wishes, Muslims affirm by large majorities their desire to live under democratic governance. For example, the "Arab Spring" is being fueled by a pro-democracy movement that wants neither the autocratic government of Hosni Mubarak nor the clerical rule of a nation such as Iran.

Substantial majorities want freedom of speech to be guaranteed in their countries and want women to have the same legal rights as men, including the rights to vote, to hold any job for which they are qualified, and to hold leadership positions in their countries. While majorities want *Shari'a* to play a role in their country and governance, only small minorities want it to be the "only source" of law.[17]

Can Islam be compatible with democracy?

Some Muslim theorists are now arguing that democracy is in fact required by Islamic theology. The doctrine that God is one (*tawhid*) and sovereign means that no person can be sovereign. Muhammad's example aids their argument: He consulted with rulers, sought the consensus of the community, reinterpreted laws when needed, and instituted programs for the welfare of the public. His successors were chosen through a process of consultation as well. In their view, this model is best followed today by a democratic style of governance.[18]

Here's the challenge: Such an argument requires Muslims to view *Shari'a* as revelation to be followed personally rather than legislation to be enforced governmentally. This is admittedly more difficult to do with the Qur'an and the *Hadith* than with the New Testament. The Christian Scriptures do not prescribe a single economic model or require particular dietary or cultural practices. *Shari'a*, by contrast, stipulates very specific actions in areas as diverse as banking and food preparation.

Some question whether Islam will ever find a way to embrace both democracy and *Shari'a*.[19] Turkish journalist and author Mustafa Akyol disagrees. In his perceptive *Islam Without Extremes: A Muslim Case for Liberty,* he makes four compelling assertions in arguing for democracy in the Muslim world.

First, the Qur'an does not prescribe a particular form of "Islamic" government after the passing of Muhammad and is "almost silent on the fundamental issues of politics."[20] Second, since Muslims are so varied in their interpretations of *Shari'a*, a democracy not built on Islamic law is the only governance fair to all. Third, only when people are free from fear of puritanical religious enforcement can they be free to choose genuine piety. Fourth, only when they are free to reject Islam can they be free to choose it.[21]

Those who are skeptical about Islam's ability to embrace democracy might remember that there was a time in the medieval Western world when the same could have been said about Christendom. An era in which church officials appointed secular rulers and enforced religious dictates in every realm of life would not have been viewed as fertile ground for democracy. The fact that large majorities of Muslims now want to live in democratic states is very hopeful.

How can we help?

America and the West should do everything we can to encourage Muslims in their movement toward democratic reform. However, such support must facilitate the only strategy that leads to genuine democracy.

Samuel Huntington (1927-2008) was one of the leading political scientists of the last 100 years. According to Francis Fukuyama, himself a noted political and social theorist, Huntington outlined three stages that lead to democratic reform.[22] The first is educational and social development, which produces a class of people seeking better jobs and lives. We see this phenomenon illustrated in Egypt, where their Human Development Index (a United Nations composite measure of income, health, and education) rose 28 percent from 1990-2010. Tens of thousands of young adults graduated from colleges, but they had no pathway to economic or political advancement. Hindered by a small group of insiders who monopolized organizational and financial control but empowered by social media, they launched what we now call the "Arab Spring."

The second stage is the creation of tools and resources necessary to functional democracy, such as a free press, labor unions, and political parties. These mechanisms then empower the third stage, a transition to free and open elections and democratic governance.

In nations that have undertaken the third stage without the second, lasting democracy has seldom been the result. For instance, the 2006 elections in Gaza empowered Hamas, which has not permitted elections since. Elections in Russia have produced a governing authority that is widely viewed as more repressive than accountable. On the other hand, following Huntington's strategy led to an effective democratic transition in Taiwan and South Korea.

It is questionable whether the tools of democracy are strong enough in Egypt, Iraq, Afghanistan, and other Muslim-majority nations to support enduring democracies. What is not in question is whether the West should do all it can to strengthen them.

Step four: Mediate peace in the Middle East

A survey of Egypt, Saudi Arabia, the United Arab Emirates, Kuwait, and Lebanon in spring 2001 announced this finding: the "majority in all five countries said that the Palestinian issue was the single most important issue to them personally."[23] Remembering that Muslims view themselves as part of an *Ummah* that transcends time and geography, what happens to one Muslim affects all Muslims. No issue is more problematic in this regard than the Israeli-Palestinian conflict.[24]

For many years it has been my privilege to lead study tours of Israel. Each time I am struck again by the tiny size of the Holy Land, a nation comparable in size to New Jersey. The country is only six miles wide at its narrowest point. And yet this postage-stamp of a nation has been pivotal to human history for four millennia.

Today the global relevance of Israel centers on its relationship with Palestine. The problem is "linkage," the term by which other problems are tied to the Israeli-Palestinian dispute. Some believe that this issue is at the heart of all our conflicts with radical Muslims. For instance, in Usama bin Laden's "Letter to America," his first example of the allegation that "you attacked us and continue to attack us" is our support for Israel.[25]

Critics of the linkage theory believe that a two-state solution would not appease radical Muslims. Groups such as Hamas would likely complain that Palestine did not receive its fair share of land so long as Israel exists at all. And they would probably undermine the treaty from within Palestine.[26]

While this may be true, there is a moral issue that should compel us to seek peace for both Israelis and Palestinians. Our Declaration of Independence claims that "all men are created equal," whatever their racial, religious, or regional status. Our solidarity with Israel is based in no small measure on our shared affirmation of universal human rights.

On my many trips to Israel, I have yet to meet an Israeli who does not believe that the Palestinians, like the Jews, deserve a homeland. Israeli and American leaders are on record affirming this commitment. The fact that radical Muslims will not cease their aggression if Palestine is granted statehood is no reason to refuse Palestinian statehood.

On one of my trips to Israel, our group was preparing to visit Bethlehem, which is located in the Palestinian-controlled West Bank. To make the 10-minute drive to the Church of the Nativity, we had to leave our Israeli-credentialed bus to board a Palestinian vehicle with its Arab driver and guide. As we were leaving one bus for the other, our Jewish tour guide saw his Palestinian counterpart. He ran to him, hugged him, and asked about his wife and children.

As the two friends clasped each other's arms, I watched with hope renewed.

Step five: Promote economic progress in the Muslim world

It surprises most Americans to learn that radical Muslims are more educated than moderates and more satisfied with their financial situations, standard of living, and quality of life. They are also more optimistic about their personal future than are moderates. However, they accuse

America of promoting chaos and civil war in their countries to steal their oil and possessions[27] and are convinced that we are oppressing their people financially.

In the Arab world, per capita income has remained virtually unchanged since 1980 while population growth has exploded. Adult literacy in Pakistan hovers at about 40 percent; rates in Egypt, Morocco, Sudan, and Yemen are closer to 50 percent.[28] It is no surprise that bin Laden would allege, "you steal our wealth and oil at paltry prices because of your international influence and military threats. This theft is indeed the biggest theft ever witnessed by mankind in the history of the world."[29] Many other radical Muslims agree that their economic deprivation is our fault and must be answered in militant terms.

Jack A. Goldstone, a professor at the George Mason School of Public Policy, recently described "four megatrends that will change the world."[30] One of them is the explosion of growth in the Muslim world. The six largest Muslim nations (Bangladesh, Egypt, Indonesia, Nigeria, Pakistan, and Turkey) grew from 242 million in 1950 to 886 million in 2009. They will exceed 1.3 billion by 2050.

Many of them will live in cities woefully unequipped to sustain them. As the world's urban population grows by three billion people by 2050, civil unrest and terrorism will likely rise. Massive cities in poor countries will generate poverty, crime lords, gangs, and rebellions. They will be less able to create or sustain democracy, and will offer abundant opportunity for recruiting terrorists.

It is in our national interest to do all we can to reverse this trend before it is too late.

Step six: Encourage moderate Muslims

When I speak on radical Islam, explaining that radical Muslims are in the vast minority in the Muslim world, inevitably someone will ask me,

"Why don't we hear from the moderate Muslims? Why don't they stand up against the radicals?"

The good news is that moderate Muslims have done more to counter the aggression of radical Islamists than most people know. Intelligence professionals with whom I have spoken on this subject tell me that their single greatest source of information in battling jihadists comes from moderate Muslim sources. While Muslims are mindful of the global *Ummah* and careful not to make statements that could be seen as critical of Islam, many have spoken and written on the need to counter radical Islam.

For example, Dr. Khaled Abou el Fadl, a professor at the UCLA School of Law, has authored a persuasive defense of moderate Islam titled *The Great Theft: Wrestling Islam From the Extremists*. He asserts that the most emphatic moral values taught by Islam are mercy, compassion, and peace.[31] In his view, the God of Islam is consistently moral and loving, "a savior and caretaker of human beings" who does not wish us to judge others on their piety or faith.[32]

He believes that Islamic law should be flexible and dynamic, not rigid and puritanical. He especially repudiates the radical Muslim's assertion that the Qur'anic verses counseling peace with non-Muslims have been supplanted by later revelation counseling self-defense and even aggression against their enemies. Dr. el Fadl correctly points out that these later revelations were all given in the context of ongoing conflict and concludes that none should be used to initiate conflict against non-aggressors. He also claims that since God is one, his character must remain the same. He could not be a God of peace in Mecca and a God of violence in Medina.[33]

Dr. el Fadl concludes:

> I believe, as the Qur'an teaches, that Islam is intended
> as a mercy for all humankind, and that the earmark of a
> Muslim is moderation. Thus Islam and Muslims should
> be the means through which all humans should see the

mercy and compassion of God demonstrated. If the two foundational values of Islam are mercy and moderation, and these foundational values are remembered and rekindled in the hearts of most Muslims, then extremism will have no quarter, and the shared pursuit of Godliness among all humankind can progress in earnest. There is no other choice.[34]

Step seven: Defend ourselves

These six steps respond to the grievances and accusations that fuel radical Islam. While the actions they recommend will be persuasive for many, others will remain unmoved, convinced that America is the "Great Satan" who must be destroyed at any cost. The tools currently at their disposal for attacking America are more frightening than ever before.

A "radiological dispersion device" or "dirty bomb" is a weapon composed of high explosives bundled with radioactive material. One such material is cesium 137, a widely available commodity typically used in dental X-rays. Such a bomb could easily kill thousands and contaminate thousands more.

A 10-kiloton nuclear bomb would obliterate three square miles and render the area uninhabitable. Such a blast in lower Manhattan would reduce our GDP by 3 percent immediately and would throw our nation into chaos. An anthrax attack would likewise kill thousands and make an area uninhabitable for months or longer.

If jihadist sleeper cells exist in America, they could launch a series of suicide attacks like the ones Israel has experienced for years. Stinger-type shoulder-fired antiaircraft missiles could bring down a passenger jet, halting commercial aviation and crippling our economy. Shipping containers that enter the United States every day are scarcely inspected and could harbor biological, chemical, or radiological weapons. Recreational airplanes can be built from kits for a few thousand dollars and converted into remote-controlled weapons. Freighters could be equipped with cruise missiles that could be launched from off our shores.[35]

In defending ourselves from future terrorism, America should make four commitments. First, we will encourage and support Israel. The Jewish state is the only true democracy in the Middle East and the one nation aligned with Western goals and values. In many ways it is our front line of defense against Middle Eastern terrorists. While we and they should work for peace with Palestine, we must continue to support Israel's right to exist and partner with her in seeking peace in the region.

Second, we will prevent a nuclear Iran. As we noted in chapter 7, Iranian president Ahmadinejad continues to threaten Israel and America. He is actively pursuing nuclear capacity that he claims will have only peaceful applications, but will not allow weapons inspectors to verify his assertions. From my travels to Israel, I can assure you that the Israeli government believes Iran to be preparing a nuclear weapon.

Former British Prime Minister Tony Blair has warned that "Iran with a nuclear bomb . . . would dramatically alter the balance of power in the region, but also within Islam."[36] Countries that are not aligned with Iran at present would find themselves threatened economically and militarily. Radical regimes such as the Syrian government and Hezbollah would be immeasurably emboldened. Israel would find herself living on the edge of nuclear war. And Iranian long-range missiles would threaten cities in Europe and perhaps the United States. In an interview with the BBC, Blair made this clear and correct pronouncement: "We need to give a message to Iran that is very clear—that they cannot have nuclear weapons capability, and we will stop them."[37]

Third, we will develop energy independence as soon as possible. At present, America imports 60 percent of her oil, 40 percent of that from OPEC (Organization of Petroleum Exporting Countries). As we have learned from past oil embargoes, "economic terrorism" is a simple and quick way to create chaos in a nation. So long as the United States relies for energy on countries vulnerable to radical Islamist agendas, we are at risk.

Fourth, we will increase our global efforts to stop jihadists before they can attack our citizens. My experiences in Israel have been illustrative in this regard. Their nation maintains remarkable vigilance. Airport security is much tighter in their country; military service is required of all Israeli youth when they turn 18 or finish the 12th grade. When our group travels through the West Bank, we always pass through numerous military checkpoints. When we return to Israel from Bethlehem, we are required to show our passports and undergo screening. Israel agrees with Thomas Jefferson that the price of freedom is eternal vigilance.

Israelis see good in the bad. They view mandatory military service as essential to maintaining their unity and common culture. They fund a significant portion of their economy through the export of technology developed for their national defense. Rather than viewing the need for perennial defense as a challenge, they seek to redeem it for greater good.

On a recent trip to Israel, one of my drivers was a veteran of the 1973 Yom Kippur War and numerous battles since. I asked him how he deals with the stress of his nation's security situation. He smiled and replied, "One day at a time." He described his home in Galilee and told me about his four daughters. "Life each day is good," he said. "If this is it—if there is to be no future for us—I am glad to have today."

Conclusion

The War on Terror requires a paradigm shift in the Western world. Rather than viewing this conflict as we have past wars, we should understand that we are engaged in an ongoing battle that crosses geographical and cultural lines. Our enemies will not rest until the entire world submits to their version of Islam. They believe that if they kill us, Allah will sort out believers from infidels in the afterlife. They believe that if we kill them, Allah will welcome them to Paradise.

According to Tony Blair, radical Islam is the greatest threat facing the world today.[38] Chuck Colson, noted political and cultural commentator, believes that our war with radical Islam "is going to go on for a hundred years."[39] But there is another way to approach this enemy. As we will see next, it is the only way that offers the promise of lasting peace.

ENDNOTES

1. John L. Esposito and Dalia Mogahed, *Who Speaks for Islam? What A Billion Muslims Really Think* (New York: Gallup Press, 2007). Other sources for this section include Mustafa Akyol, *Islam Without Extremes: A Muslim Case for Liberty* (New York: W. W. Norton & Company, 2011); Daniel Benjamin and Steven Simon, *The Age of Sacred Terror: Radical Islam's War Against America* (New York: Random House, 2003); John L. Esposito, *Unholy War: Terror In the Name of Islam* (New York: Oxford University Press, 2002); Khaled Abou el Fadl, *The Great Theft: Wrestling Islam from the Extremists* (New York: HarperOne, 2007); Seyyed Hossein Nasr, *Islam in the Modern World: Challenged By the West, Threatened by Fundamentalism, Keeping Faith with Tradition* (New York: HarperOne, 2010); Monica Duffy Toft, Daniel Philpott, and Timothy Samuel Shah, *God's Century: Resurgent Religion and Global Politics* (New York: W. W. Norton & Company, 2011); and Lawrence Wright, *The Looming Tower: Al-Qaeda and the Road to 9-11* (New York: Vintage Books, 2006).

2. Esposito and Mogahed 69.

3. Germany's military comprised 18.2 million soldiers; Japan military numbered 6.1 million; Italy's military totaled nearly 4 million soldiers.

4. Esposito and Mogahed 90.

5. http://www.time.com/time/specials/packages/article/0,28804,2036683_2037181_2037470,00.html, accessed 18 July 2011.

6. Serbian historian Serge Trifkovic, quoted in Kerby Anderson *A Biblical Point of View on Islam* (Eugene, Oregon: Harvest House Publishers, 2008) 101.

7. Benjamin and Simon 419.

8. Esposito and Mogahed 71-2.

9. Wright 39-42.

10. For a definitive study of America's historic role in the Middle East, see Michael B. Oren, *Power, Faith, and Fantasy: America in the Middle East 1776 to the Present* (New York: W. W. Norton & Company, 2007).

11. For discussion of commonalities among religious fundamentalist groups and movements, see Esposito, *Unholy War*, 151; Benjamin and Simon, 422-46; Toft, Philpott, and Shah, 123ff; and Esposito and Mogahed, 76.

12. Esposito and Mogahed 77, 79.

13.   Ibid., 82-9.

14.   Esposito, *Unholy War*, 160.

15.   Esposito and Mogahed, 80.

16.   Ibid., 30, 39.

17.   Ibid., 47, 51, 48.

18.   Esposito, *Unholy War*, 145.

19.   See, for example, Ibn Warraq, *Why I Am Not A Muslim* (Amherst, New York: Prometheus Books, 2003 [1995]) 172-92.

20.   Akyol 250.

21.   Ibid., 247-86.

22.   Francis Fukuyama, "Political Order in Egypt," *The American Interest* May-June 2011 (http://www.the-american-interest.com/article.cfm?piece=953), accessed 18 July 2011.

23.   Esposito, *Unholy War*, 154.

24.   For an in-depth analysis of peace efforts across history and religious divides, see Toft, Philpott, and Shah, pp. 174-206.

25.   http://www.guardian.co.uk/world/2002/nov/24/theobserver, accessed 18 July 2011.

26.   See, for example, James Kirchick, "The Broken Link: What Peace Won't Fix," *World Affairs*, July/August 2010 (http://www.worldaffairsjournal.org/articles/2010-JulyAugust/full-Kirchick-JA-2010.html), accessed 18 July 2011.

27.   Esposito and Mogahed 71-2, 82.

28.   Benjamin and Simon 176-8.

29.   http://www.guardian.co.uk/world/2002/nov/24/theobserver, accessed 18 July 2011.

30.   Jack A. Goldstone, "The New Population Bomb: The Four Megatrends That Will Change the World," *Foreign Affairs*, vol. 89 no. 1 (January/February 2010) 31-43.

31.   El Fadl 11.

32.   Ibid., 135.

33.   Ibid., 203-19.

34.   Ibid., 288.

35.   Benjamin and Simon 397-400, 477-9.

36.   Tony Blair, *A Journey: My Political Life* (New York: Alfred A. Knopf, 2010) 666.

37.   http://www.bbc.co.uk/news/world-11182225, accessed 18 July 2011.

38.   http://www.bbc.co.uk/news/world-11182225, accessed 18 July 2011.

39.   Quoted in Anderson 109.

CHAPTER NINE

WHERE WAS GOD ON 9/11?

SPIRITUAL IMPLICATIONS OF THE WAR ON TERROR

My first visit to Pearl Harbor was a sobering experience I will never forget. Standing over the sunken USS *Arizona* with her 1,102 entombed servicemen, I watched as oil seeping from the ship surfaced on the calm Pacific waters. The droplets are called "the tears of the Arizona."

The memorial to those who died on September 11, 2001, is very different. Skyscrapers are being erected where the Twin Towers once stood. A vision of vibrant freedom is coming more to life as each day passes. But many of us who remember that terrible morning still wonder where God was on the day the towers came down.

In this final chapter, let's ask some hard but important questions about Christianity and radical Islam.

Why does God allow terrorism?

We watched in horror on that Tuesday morning while Americans jumped to their deaths from burning towers. We cringed at images of the Pentagon smoldering and Flight 93 scattered across the Pennsylvania soil. If God is all-knowing, he saw the 9/11 plot being formed and knew what would happen on that fateful day. If he is all-loving, he would not want innocent people to fall victim to senseless terror. If he is all-powerful, he could prevent their deaths. Yet he did not.

To some, 9/11 is proof that the God of the Bible is a myth. For example, Christopher Hitchens is convinced that "religion poisons everything," the subtitle of his bestselling diatribe.[1] It was my privilege to engage in a panel debate with him a few years ago. I found him gracious off the stage and acerbic on it. During our debate he repeatedly pointed to innocent suffering as proof that God could not exist.

There are other ways to answer our question. The Bible repeatedly emphasizes the fact that God created humans with free will so we could choose to love him and others. When we misuse this freedom, the consequences are not his fault but ours.

God did not choose for the 9/11 terrorists to plan and execute their attack on Americans. The God who is love (1 John 4:8) forbids murder (Exodus 20:13). If he removed the consequences of our freedom, however, he would remove our freedom. He could have prevented 9/11, but to be fair he would have to prevent the results of all other misused freedom as well.

Instead, he grieves with his children in our suffering. The One who wept beside the grave of Lazarus (John 11:35) weeps beside every grave dug because of terrorism. The Father knows what it is to lose a Son and feels the pain of every family grieving today.

Elie Wiesel's books told the world of the Holocaust atrocities he survived. No passage is more horrifying than his account of a small boy hanged by the Nazis:

For more than half an hour he stayed there, struggling between life and death, dying in slow agony under our eyes. And we had to look him full in the face. He was still alive when I passed in front of him. His tongue was still red, his eyes were not yet glazed. Behind me, I heard [a] man asking: "Where is God now?" And I heard a voice within me answer him: "Where is He? Here He is—He is hanging here on this gallows . . ."[2]

While God grieves our suffering, he redeems all that he allows. Just as he redeemed his Son's death for the salvation of all who trust in him, so he redeems all evil and suffering for a greater good. Sometimes we can see that good on this side of heaven, but often we cannot.

So it is with the tragedy of 9/11. Millions turned to God in prayer in the days after the tragedy; many came to faith in Christ while others grew stronger in their commitment. He did not cause the horror of that day or acts of terrorism since, but he continues to use them for good.

Why are Muslims coming to Christ?

One way God has used 9/11 is to mobilize Christians around the world to reach out to Muslims. It is not a coincidence that more Muslims are coming to faith in Christ today than at any time in Islamic history. For instance, Saudi Arabian Sheikh Ahmad al-Qatanni reported on al-Jazeera television that every day, "16,000 Muslims convert to Christianity." He claimed that Islam was losing six million followers a year to Christian faith.[3] While he could be inflating his numbers to incite Islamic reaction against Christianity, it is clear that a significant Christian movement is occurring in the Muslim world, much of it coming in the years following 9/11.

Why are so many Muslims turning to Christ as their Lord? One answer is visions and dreams. Muslims already have a very high view of Jesus (*Isa* in the Arabic). The Qur'an teaches that Jesus was born of a virgin: "[Mary] said: 'O my Lord! How shall I have a son when no man hath touched me?'" (Qur'an 3:47). They believe that her Son possessed the miraculous ability to "speak to the people in childhood and in maturity" and would be in the sinless company of the "righteous" (3:46). He would "heal those born blind, and the lepers, and . . . quicken the dead, by God's leave" (3:49). And God would "take thee and raise thee to myself" (3:55).

Now this One whom they believe to be the virgin-born, sinless son of Mary in heaven is using dreams and visions to bring Muslims around the world to himself. Dr. Abraham Sarker is an example. While in Bangladesh, he dreamed of himself in hell and heard a voice instruct him to "go and get a Bible." When he came to America as a missionary for Islam, he read a Bible for the first time, met Christians, and eventually came to faith in Jesus.[4]

Thousands of Muslims around the globe are reporting similar miraculous experiences.[5] I met one such person in Bangladesh. Shortly after her father died he appeared to her in a dream, instructing her to go to a specific house in their village where a man had a message she needed to hear. Her father showed her the face of this person, an American she had never met.

The next morning she made her way to the house and was shocked to find the very man in her dream speaking to a group of people. His name is Harold Sadler, a well-known Christian businessman in the Dallas area and frequent traveler to Bangladesh. After he finished, she introduced herself and asked what message he had for her. Harold had no idea what she was talking about. After she explained her dream, he shared the Christian gospel with her and she became a follower of Jesus. She ran home to bring her daughter and son, who became Christians that day as well. I was introduced to her when we visited her village and found her faith to be vibrant and joyful.

Christians can pray for Muslims around the world to meet Jesus in such dreams and visions. And we can share his love with Muslims in America and around the world. In this way we help people who might be influenced by the hatred of radical Islam to experience instead the hope found in Christ.

What else can Christians do?

When visiting Bangladesh recently, I met my first radical Muslim. He was a teacher at one of the village *madrassas*. Our group, led by Dr. Sarker, came to the school for a tour that the *madrassa*'s leader kindly arranged. He invited us into his office, where we sat on the floor in a circle and exchanged the pleasantries that are common to their gracious culture.

From the beginning, one of his faculty was visibly frustrated by our presence. As soon as there was a pause in our conversation he burst in with a long, impassioned speech. As Dr. Sarker began translating the teacher's angry words into English, he whispered to me that I must not respond to him. It became harder to obey my friend's request as time went on.

The teacher lambasted Christianity as a false religion with a flawed book and insisted that we must all convert to Islam if we wished to go to heaven. He made it clear that we were not welcome in his village and intimated threats if we did not leave. I learned later that he had been responsible for recent violence against others in the area. While I earnestly wanted to answer his false statements and offer him the grace of Christ, Dr. Sarker knew that any response on my part would be perceived as aggression and met in kind. Two days later, we learned that this man's rudeness had so embarrassed the leader of the *madrassa* that he removed him from his position and transferred him to a distant village.

Meeting this man gave me firsthand experience with the opposition Muslims face when they convert to Christianity. As angry as he was with me, I can only imagine his animosity toward Muslims who leave his faith for mine. "Muslim-background believers" (MBBs) often face such ridicule and rejection from their families and cultures. Many lose their possessions, while some lose their lives.

When they leave Islam for Christianity, MBBs find themselves without a faith-family. Very little about American churches is familiar to them. Imagine yourself trying to learn how to worship in a Buddhist temple or Jewish synagogue and you can sympathize with their plight. Their Muslim prayers had been ritual performances; now they must learn to pray to God from their hearts. Their Muslim Scriptures have rejected the Bible as outdated and flawed; now they must learn how to study its truths. Their Muslim leaders may have characterized Christians as "Crusaders" and enemies of Islam; now they must join them in worship and service.

Several organizations in the United States exist to support MBBs; I recommend especially Dr. Sarker's ministry, Gospel For Muslims.[6] By visiting their website and attending their conferences, you will meet MBBs and discover ways you can help them to grow in Christ and share their faith with the Muslim world.

What is God doing in our world?

A "great awakening" is defined by historians as a spiritual movement that transforms cultures and nations. There have been four such movements in Western history: in 1734 (often called "the Great Awakening"), in 1792, in 1858, and in 1904-5 (sometimes called the "Welsh Revival").

Now there is a fifth Great Awakening occurring in our world. According to David Barrett, author of the *World Christian Encyclopedia,* 72,900 people become Christians every day. More are coming to Christ than at any time in Christian history. In Africa, 24,000 will become followers of Jesus today; 19,400 in Asia; and 21,000 today in Latin America.[7]

Another recent study of this phenomenon claims that the numbers of new Christians are far higher than Barrett documents. John Micklethwait is editor in chief of *The Economist*; his writing partner, Adrian Wooldridge, is its Washington bureau chief and columnist. One is Roman Catholic, the other an atheist; both are Oxford graduates. In *God Is Back: How the Global*

Revival of Faith is Changing the World,[8] they describe this staggering spiritual awakening sweeping the world. Facts about the global explosion of Christian faith:

- A million people become Christians every week, the largest number in history.
- In 1900 there were roughly 10 million Christians in Africa; today there are 400 million, 45 percent of the population.
- Yoido Full Gospel Church in Seoul, South Korea, began in a tent in 1956 and now claims 830,000 members; 3,000 join every week. Five of the 10 largest churches in the world are in South Korea.
- Pentecostalism, founded in a Los Angeles ghetto in 1906, now claims 500 million followers around the world.
- In 1900, 80 percent of the world's Christians lived in Europe and the United States; today, 60 percent live in the developing world. More Roman Catholics attend church in the Philippines than in Italy. Churches in the developing world now export 100,000 missionaries.

Are we missing this movement of God?

Of the 72,900 daily conversions documented by Barrett, only 7,200 are in Europe and North America, combined. While much of the world is experiencing an explosion in Christian growth, Americans are living in a time of unprecedented skepticism with regard to historic Christianity.

According to the latest American Religious Identification Survey, the number of Americans who describe themselves as "Christian" has dropped from 86 percent to 76 percent since 1990. At the same time, the number who say they have "no religion" has nearly doubled to more than 15 percent.

The number who call themselves "atheist" or "agnostic" has quadrupled and is now almost twice the number of Episcopalians in our country.[9]

The Pew Forum on Religion and Public Life recently released their "U.S. Religious Landscape Survey." Among its findings:

- More than one-quarter of American adults (28 percent) have left the faith in which they were raised in favor of another religion or no religion at all.
- Among Americans ages 18-29, one in four says he is not affiliated with any religion.[10]

Spiritual trends in Europe are even more discouraging. A recent Harris Poll conducted a large survey of religious beliefs in France, Germany, Great Britain, Italy, Spain, and the U.S. What percentage of the various populations believes in "any form of God or any type of supreme being"? According to the survey, 62 percent in Italy, 48 percent in Spain, 41 percent in Germany, 35 percent in England, and 27 percent in France believe in God by any definition.[11]

In Great Britain today, there are four times as many Muslims attending mosque on Friday as Christians attending worship on Sunday. Twenty-five percent of Brussels is Muslim. Fifty-four million Muslims live in Europe; their numbers will continue to increase due to immigration and high birth rates.

Micklethwait and Wooldridge document these facts about the demise of Christianity in Europe:

- A century ago, Britain had the same level of religious commitment as the United States. Half of children under 15 years of age were enrolled in Sunday School. Today, 6 percent of Britons attend church on an average Sunday.

- On current trends, the Church of England will lose more than half that attendance in the next 20 years and be forced to close another 6,000 churches. Fifty-eight percent of churchgoers in London are non-Anglo immigrants.
- In a 2004 survey, 44 percent of Britons claimed that they had no religious identification whatsoever. Two-thirds of people age 18 to 24 call themselves nonreligious; almost half of these young adults don't believe that Jesus existed as a historical figure.
- One in 20 people in France attends a religious service once a week. Five percent in Sweden attend weekly worship services; fewer than 2 percent in Denmark attend church regularly.
- Meanwhile, a mega-mosque planned for east London will hold 12,000 people, five times as many as St. Paul's Cathedral. In 2008, London's new mayor helped organize a festival in Trafalgar Square to celebrate the end of Ramadan. The mayors of Rotterdam and Leicester are Muslims.

What do we know about the current state of American Christianity? According to Micklethwait and Wooldridge,

- Fewer than half of Americans can name the first book of the Bible.
- Only a third know who delivered the Sermon on the Mount (Billy Graham is a popular answer).
- A quarter do not know what is celebrated at Easter.
- Sixty percent cannot name half the Ten Commandments.

The simple fact is, where the fifth Great Awakening is in the ascent, Islam is in the decline. Where nations are missing the Awakening, Islam is growing—often in numbers that far outstrip the rest of the population.

Does democracy require morality?

If you could fix one problem in America today, what would it be? A recent survey asked a large number of Americans that question. Their first answer was, "restoring national economic stability." That's no surprise in these days of recession. But tying for first, ahead of "preventing terrorism" and "curing cancer," was: "restoring values and morality to society."[12]

Why are values and morality so important to our nation's future?

Plato, one of the greatest minds in human history, was convinced that a democracy could not last. The people could be swayed too easily by public speakers, he warned. And once the people discovered that they could vote based on their personal interests rather than the good of the nation, their democracy would begin to fail.

Are his warnings coming true today?

Americans live in a society that says that you have no right to force your beliefs on anyone else. Morality is a matter of personal preference. So long as I don't hurt anyone, I should be free to live as I please. Values and morality are subjective and private.

But imagine for a moment what would happen if Americans chose to live by biblical morality. For instance, the Bible says that sex outside of marriage is wrong. No standard could seem more outdated and irrelevant in our society. But what would happen if we lived by this one simple principle?

The United States has the highest teen pregnancy rate in the industrialized world. The Centers for Disease Control say that one-third of girls in America become pregnant before the age of 20; 81 percent of them are unmarried.[13] More than 100,000 websites offer illegal child pornography. Approximately 90 percent of 8-16 year olds have viewed porn online, most while doing their homework.[14] How would living by biblical sexual morality change our nation with respect to teenage pregnancy, abortion, and pornography?

The Bible says that stealing is wrong. Over $15 billion is lost each year in America due to employee theft.[15] In 2008 more than 9.9 million Americans were victims of identity theft, our nation's fastest growing crime, at a cost of $48 billion.[16] Imagine a nation that lived by the biblical command not to steal.

Josh McDowell, a well-known specialist on youth issues, warns that we may be living in America's "last Christian generation."[17] Here are facts supporting his assertion:

- Between 69 percent and 94 percent of youth leave the traditional church after high school.
- Sixty-three percent don't believe Jesus is the Son of the one true God; 58 percent believe all faiths teach equally valid truths; 51 percent don't believe Jesus rose from the dead; 65 percent don't believe Satan is a real entity; and 68 percent don't believe the Holy Spirit is real.
- When young people do not adopt a foundational Christian belief system, they are 48 percent more likely to cheat on an exam; 200 percent more likely to steal; 300 percent more likely to use illegal drugs; and 600 percent more likely to attempt suicide.
- Sixty-five percent of church-attending youth believe that there is "no way to tell which religion is true." Seventy percent believe there is no absolute moral truth.
- The most common reason cited by young people who fall away from church is "intellectual skepticism."
- 3.5 million adolescents suffer from depression each year; 2,000 take their lives, while another 1,000 make attempts so serious that they require medical attention.

In a democracy we do not seek to legislate morality. But did the founders of our nation believe that morality was essential to their democratic experiment?

In his farewell address (September 19, 1796), President George Washington told the nation: "Of all the dispositions and habits which lead to political prosperity, Religion and morality are indispensable supports. . . . Reason and experience both forbid us to expect that National morality can prevail in exclusion of religious principle. . . . Virtue or morality is a necessary spring of popular government."[18]

John Adams, our second president, claimed that "the general principles on which the fathers achieved independence were the general principles of Christianity." He stated, "Suppose a nation in some distant Region should take the Bible for their only law Book and every member should regulate his conduct by the precepts there exhibited. . . . What a Eutopia, what a Paradise would this region be."[19]

Speaking six years before the beginning of the Great Recession, an economic calamity brought on by corporate greed, President George W. Bush made this perceptive statement: "All investment is an act of faith, and faith is earned by integrity. In the long run, there's no capitalism without conscience; there is no wealth without character."[20]

Do we need a King?

In the Bible, God is a King. Jesus began his public ministry with the call to "repent, for the kingdom of heaven is at hand" (Matthew 4:17). He taught us to "seek first his kingdom and his righteousness, and all these things will be given to you as well" (Matthew 6:33). He instructed us to pray, "your kingdom come, your will be done on earth as it is in heaven" (Matthew 6:10). When he returns, his name will be "King of Kings and Lord of Lords" (Revelation 19:16).

By contrast, in our culture God is a hobby. Our cultural roots are not found in the soil of Scripture but the mountains of Greece. There we learned that the gods live atop Mount Olympus, remote and irrelevant to our daily lives. If we make offerings at their temples they will bless our crops, give us victory in battle, or grant whatever else we ask. Transactional religion was the order of the day.

It still is for many Western Christians. Go to church on Sunday so God will bless you on Monday. Give money so he will bless you financially. Start your day with Bible study and prayer so he will bless your day. Give to him so he will give to you.

And keep your faith and life separate. In our culture religion is a private, personal, subjective experience. Like any other hobby, we have no right to force it on others. So long as you're sincere in your faith and tolerant of mine we'll all get along.

But if God is a king, you're wearing his clothes. You're breathing his air and standing on his planet. Every day is his, not just Sunday. Every moment is his, not just those you spend in church. Every dollar is his, not just those you put in an offering plate. Everything you do is accountable to him, not just what the rest of us see. He wants not a transactional religion but a transformational relationship with you.

All around the world today, people are making God their King. In 2010 South Korean churches sent more missionaries into the world than America did. There is a worship movement sweeping Australia and contemporary churches around the world. A Christian revival is happening on the African continent, where Christian growth is outstripping Islam. In southern Nigeria, for instance, 90 percent of the people are in church on Sundays. (In America, if you call our churches and total their attendance, it comes to 23 percent of the population).

When I was in Beijing recently, I was told that 100,000 people come to Christ every day in the People's Republic of China. When I last preached in Cuba, we watched 330 people make public professions of faith on a single Sunday morning. The reason was not my preaching; the day before, 294 Cuban Christians knocked on 1,050 doors in their community and shared their faith with 5,000 of their neighbors. The next morning, more people responded to the gospel than I have ever seen on a single day. To the Cubans this was nothing unusual—more than a million have become Christians in the last decade.

The most important way Christians can join the War on Terror is on our knees.

Conclusion

I once heard Rick Warren say, "Stop asking God to bless what you are doing, and ask him to help you do what he is blessing." What God Almighty is blessing is a global spiritual awakening, a movement of the Holy Spirit wherever people make him their King. That is what God is doing in these days.

Will you join him? Will you admit that your church and community and nation needs more of God than you have known? Do you need to experience the power of God, a transforming spiritual movement? Will you admit your need of God and humble yourself before him? Will you seek to glorify him with everything you think and say and do this week? Will you pray every day for spiritual awakening to come to America, starting with you?

There is no time to waste.

If you were asked to name the world's greatest military, strongest economy, and largest empire in the year 1900, the answer would be Great Britain. If you were asked to guess the army with the most troops, tanks, artillery, and nuclear weapons in 1980, the answer would be the Soviet Union.

Emerson insisted, "One of our illusions is that the present hour is not the crucial hour." He was right. We don't have another year or another day to wait. The hour is upon us. We must seek awakening while there is still time. Tomorrow is promised to no nation, including ours.

I have taped these words on the inside of my Bible where I can see them each day: "There is one thing that must never be forgotten. It is as if a king had sent you to a foreign country with a task to perform. You go and perform many other tasks. But if you fail to perform the task for which you were sent, it will be as if you had done nothing at all."

In responding to the threat of radical Islam, what does your King ask of you?

ENDNOTES

1. Christopher Hitchens, *god is Not Great: How Religion Poisons Everything* (New York: Hatchette Book Group USA, 2007).

2. Elie Wiesel, *Night,* Modern Critical Interpretations, edited with an introduction by Harold Bloom (New York: Chelsea House, 2001) 13.

3. http://www.nairaland.com/nigeria/topic-523588.0.html, accessed 25 July 2011.

4. See Dr. Sarker's testimony at http://www.gospelformuslims.com/mbb_testimonies.php.

5. For examples, go to http://www.30-days.net/testimony/dreams/ and http://www.truthnet.org/dreamsandvisions/.

6. http://www.gospelformuslims.com/, accessed 25 July 2011.

7. http://www.bible.ca/global-religion-statistics-world-christian-encyclopedia.htm, accessed 25 July 2011.

8. John Micklethwait and Adrian Wooldridge, *God is Back: How the Global Revival of Faith is Changing the World* (New York: The Penguin Press, 2009).

9. livinginliminality.files.wordpress.com/2009/03/aris_report_2008.pdf, accessed 25 July 2011.

10. http://religions.pewforum.org/reports, accessed 25 July 2011.

11. http://www.harrisinteractive.com/news/allnewsbydate.asp?NewsID=1131, accessed 25 July 2011.

12. Frank I. Luntz, *What Americans Really Want . . . Really: The Truth About Our Hopes, Dreams, and Fears* (New York: Hyperion) 288.

13. http://www.livestrong.com/article/12504-teen-pregnancy-rates-usa/, accessed 25 July 2011.

14. http://healthymind.com/s-porn-stats.html, accessed 25 July 2011.

15. http://www.usaspecialservicesllc.com/background.htm, accessed 25 July 2011.

16. http://www.bytecrime.org/stats.php, accessed 25 July 2011.

17. Josh McDowell, *The Last Christian Generation* (Holiday, Florida: Green Key Books, 2006).

18. http://www.earlyamerica.com/earlyamerica/milestones/farewell/, accessed 25 July 2011.

19. http://christianity.about.com/od/independenceday/a/foundingfathers.htm, accessed 25 July 2011.

20. http://archives.cnn.com/2002/ALLPOLITICS/07/09/bush.transcript/index.html, accessed 25 July 2011.

How Do We Win the War on Terror? Three Steps to Take Today

What will historians call the military conflict in which we have been engaged since 2001? While addressing a joint session of Congress and the American people nine days after 9/11, President George W. Bush called this battle the "War on Terror," the name most use today.[1] The Obama administration prefers the term "Overseas Contingency Operations."[2] Conservative historian Norman Podhoretz calls it "World War IV" (World War III being the Cold War).[3]

Today many prefer the description, "The Long War."[4] In June 2010, after 104 months of combat, the war in Afghanistan passed the Vietnam War as the longest military engagement in United States history. President Obama has announced plans to remove our troops by 2012, a goal that some critics believe is unlikely to be met. Even if U.S. battle forces are gone from Iraq and Afghanistan in a few years, our conflict with radical Muslims will be far from over.

We have never fought an enemy that is engaged on so many fronts—Egypt, Israel, Lebanon, Yemen, Iraq, Iran, Afghanistan, Pakistan, and the list continues to grow. Small cadres of passionate jihadists can wreak havoc on our cities and economy. This is an enemy with no single leader we can kill and no single land we can capture. Our conflict with radical Islam was the first war of the 21st century and is likely to be the longest.

But there are steps we can take to win this war. None are easy or simple, but all are urgent.

Step one: Do more

"Despite nearly a decade of war, al Qaeda is stronger today than when it carried out the 9/11 attacks." So states Leah Farrell, a former Counterterrorism Intelligence Analyst with the Australian Federal Police.[5]

There is no question that our military response in Afghanistan forced bin Laden to flee to Pakistan and severely weakened his organization there. But he responded by activating a franchise of al-Qaeda in the Arabian Peninsula (AQAP), led by Ayman al-Awlaki and charged with carrying out attacks against America. A second branch was created in Iraq to undermine democracy there. A third franchise was created in the Maghreb, the western region of North Africa that includes Morocco, Algeria, Tunisia, Libya, and Mauritania. A fourth works with the Abdullah Azzam Brigades in Lebanon. Al-Qaeda also operates al-Shabaab, a youth movement in Somalia, Islamic Jihad in Egypt, and the East Turkestan Islamic Movement in Xinjiang, China.

As a result, the terror organization has secured greater reach than ever before in its history. FBI Director Robert Mueller told a hearing of the

Senate Homeland Security and Governmental Affairs Committee in September 2010, "Despite the significant counterterrorism pressure abroad, al Qaeda continues to be committed to high-profile attacks directed at the West, including plans against Europe as well as the homeland."[6] According to Michael Leiter, director of the National Counterterrorism Center, 2010 brought the largest number and fastest pace of attempted attacks since September 11.[7]

Our investment in this war continues to mount. According to the Center for Defense Information, the United States spent $171 billion on the War on Terror in 2010.[8] We have spent $75 billion on intelligence and have constructed 33 new building complexes for intelligence bureaucracies. And we spend $3.4 billion to house the Department of Homeland Security, which has a workforce of 230,000 people.[9]

Despite these monumental efforts, the claims of radical Islam continue to find followers around the world. In 2009, Khaled Sheikh Mohammed and four other prisoners at the Guantanamo Bay detention facility released a statement in which they claimed with pride their roles in 9/11. They thanked God that they were "terrorists to the bone" and explained their actions: "We fight you over defending Muslims, their land, their holy sites, and their religion as a whole."[10]

A 2008 study by the RAND Corporation discovered that among all 648 terrorist groups in its data set, only 41 percent have ended their activities. The study noted that of the religious terrorist groups that have ended operations, 57 percent did so only because they splintered into other groups. Approximately 29 percent were defeated through local police actions, while only seven percent fell to military force and another seven percent shifted toward non-violent political activity.[11]

Clearly, what we are doing is not ending our war with radical Islam. But according to geopolitical expert George Friedman, there's a reason we've fought the War on Terror as we have. He believes that our strategy is consistent with our nation's "metanarrative," its overarching definition of success. Since achieving superpower status, the United States' global priority has been to preserve this position.[12]

Friedman argues that our engagements since World War II have been designed primarily to defend our international role and position. In this view, we fought in Korea and Vietnam to prevent communist forces from dominating these regions and threatening our global interests. "Victory" was not defined as it was in the world wars. Our purpose was not to defeat an enemy that threatened our nation so much as it was to contain a rival power lest it ascend in global reach.[13]

Seen this way, our military engagements in Iraq and Afghanistan accomplish their purpose so long as al-Qaeda and other militant groups do not become a pan-Muslim coalition that could achieve superpower status. When we believe that the Iraqi and Afghan governments can continue this work without our support, we will withdraw our forces. But our objective is not to defeat radical Islam—only to contain it.

If this strategy is indeed motivating our conduct of the War on Terror, it is based on a flawed definition of success. Unlike previous enemies who fought conventional wars for conventional purposes, jihadists seek nothing less than global conquest for militant Islam. A single terrorist can disrupt an industry or economy. Small groups can destroy skyscrapers. It is not enough to contain them; we must defeat them.

For example, a containment strategy against this enemy puts the United States at continued economic risk. There is no doubt that oil is the gold of today's global economy. The United States has an estimated 29.9 billion barrels of reserves, ranking 11th in the world. The top five nations (in order) are Saudi Arabia, Iran, Iraq, Kuwait, and the United Arab Emirates. They possess a combined 716 billion barrels, 60 percent of the world's supply. If militant regimes were to come to power in these nations, they could shut off our oil and cripple our economy.

And a containment strategy dooms us to continue fighting a war of attrition with an enemy who only has to survive to win. Henry Kissinger was right: "A design for simply maintaining the present security situation runs the risk of confirming the adage that guerrillas win if they do not lose."[14]

Step two: Win the culture war

When sociologist James Davison Hunter coined the phrase "culture war" in 1991, he was speaking of American conflicts over the family, art, education, law, and politics.[15] But his term effectively describes our conflict with radical Islam as well.

As we have seen, our enemies believe passionately that killing Americans is a defense of Islam required by the Qur'an. So long as they can accuse us of oppressing them politically, economically, and morally, they will do so. We cannot meet their demands without abandoning Israel and our other friends in the Middle East, ceasing our export of oil from their lands, and surrendering our people and future to their extremist view of Islam. But we can take steps to make their rhetoric less appealing to the larger Muslim world.

My point is not related to the seven percent who are already radicalized. These enemies must be opposed with force unless they change their spiritual ideology (see step three). But we can and should focus on Muslims who are potential recruits to their cause. Only by winning their minds can we win this war.

As we saw in chapter 8, the West can take significant steps toward strengthening our relationship with the larger Muslim world. We can build bridges with non-radical Muslim leaders, enlisting their help as we battle an enemy who threatens them as much as it menaces us. We can wage peace in the Middle East, help build democracy, and engage in economic renewal. So long as jihadist organizations such as Hamas and Hezbollah do more for their people than Israel and the West, they will gain popular support for their causes.

And we can utilize the technological tools of radical Muslims against them. For years militants have made the Internet their primary recruiting ground. Jihadist websites proliferate with virtually no accountability. It is time we turned the tables.[16]

First, we should show Muslims around the world that jihadists are their enemies. Religious insurgents in Iraq killed 95,000-105,000 innocent civilians between March 2003 and the end of 2009, out of a total civilian death count of 110,600. By contrast, some 5,000 civilian deaths were inadvertently caused by coalition forces. There is no question that the first victims of radical Muslims are fellow Muslims. We have not done enough to make this fact clear to the world. Fewer Muslims would join a movement to liberate Islam that victimizes Muslims.

Second, we should expose the non-Islamic tactics of jihadists. The Qur'an permits aggression only against combatants (9:13; 22:38-39), a doctrine that radical Muslims consistently violate. The concept that citizens of a nation are complicit in every decision made by their leaders is inconsistent with historic Islamic theology. No one in al-Qaeda or other terror organizations possesses sufficient religious training or credentials to legitimize such a theological pronouncement. If Muslims could see jihadists as illegitimate spiritually, they would refuse to join their movement to "defend Islam."

Third, we should show the Muslim world that jihadist groups have no answers for their real problems. "The solution is Islam" is a persuasive creed, but it is not a governing strategy. Few in the Muslim world want to live in a repressed, backward, Taliban-like society. Even radicalized Muslims admire the technology, democracy, and gender equality of the West.[17] When we offer a vision of the future that meets their most essential needs and hopes, we give them a reason to reject militant Islam.

The Muslim world continues to explode demographically around the world. The Muslim birthrate in European nations is three times higher than the non-Muslim one.[18] Many speak of Europe's future as "Eurabia."[19] The sooner we adopt a clear and motivated strategy to counter radical Islam in the Muslim world, the sooner we will end this war.

Step three: Engage spiritually

I have written this book to help all Americans understand radical Islam and do not assume that its readers are Christians. For those who are, a third step in winning the War on Terror is imperative: join this battle spiritually.

As we have seen, more than 100 million Muslims have already been radicalized. Western governments can and should engage in strategies intended to counter their commitment to their militant cause, but such tactics have not proven successful with the large majority of jihadists.[20]

However, as we noted in chapter 9, a very hopeful spiritual movement is sweeping the Muslim world. Multiplied thousands of Muslims are meeting Jesus in dreams and visions, and many are turning to him as their Lord. Among them are Muslims previously committed to a radical ideology that wages war against Christians. Their transformations are eternally significant, of course, but they are also highly relevant to the War on Terror.

If you are a Christian, I urge you to join me in praying daily for Muslims to find the hope of Christ. Ask your pastor and church to join you. As thousands of American women and men risk their lives to defend us from our enemies, we can join them on battlefields where the weapons are spiritual: "our struggle is not against flesh and blood, but against the rulers, against the authorities, against the powers of this dark world and against the spiritual forces of evil in the heavenly realms" (Ephesians 6:12).

My grandfather risked his life to defend America in World War I. My father nearly died on a South Pacific island, defending our nation in World War II. Now we are engaged in the battle of this generation. Will history find us faithful?

ENDNOTES

1. http://www.historyplace.com/speeches/gw-bush-9-11.htm, accessed 20 July 2011.

2. http://www.washingtonpost.com/wp-dyn/content/article/2009/03/24/AR2009032402818.html, accessed 20 July 2011.

3. Norman Podhoretz, *World War IV: The Long Struggle Against Islamofascism* (New York: Doubleday, 2007).

4. http://www.washingtonpost.com/wp-dyn/content/article/2006/02/02/AR2006020202242.html, accessed 20 July 2011.

5. Leah Farrall, "How al Qaeda works," *Foreign Affairs* March/April 2011 http://www.foreignaffairs.com/articles/67467/leah-farrall/how-al-qaeda-works, accessed 20 July 2011.

6. http://www.acus.org/natosource/europe-faces-higher-threat-al-qaeda, accessed 20 July 2011.

7. http://www.weeklystandard.com/blogs/leiter-terrorist-attacks-surpassed-number-and-pace-attacks-during-any-year-911, accessed 20 July 2011.

8. http://www.infoplease.com/ipa/A0933935.html, accessed 20 July 2011.

9. http://www.newsweek.com/2010/09/04/zakaria-why-america-overreacted-to-9-11.html, accessed 20 July 2011.

10. Quoted in Monica Duffy Toft, Daniel Philpott, and Timothy Samuel Shah, *God's Century: Resurgent Religion and Global Politics* (New York: W. W. Norton and Company, 2011), 121.

11. Ibid., 144.

12. George Friedman, *The Next 100 Years: A Forecast for the 21st Century* (London: Allison & Busby Limited, 2009) 15-32.

13. Ibid., 21.

14. http://www.henryakissinger.com/articles/wp121805.html, accessed 20 July 2011.

15. James Davison Hunter, *Culture Wars: The Struggle to Define America* (n.p., Basic Books, 1991).

16. The following strategies are described and defended well in Carl Ciovanno, Howard Gambrill Clark and James Van de Velde, *Ending al-Qaeda*, "The American Interest," July/August 2011, 40-9.

17. John L. Esposito and Dalia Mogahed, *Who Speaks for Islam? What a Billion Muslims Really Think* (New York: Gallup Press, 2007) 80.

18. http://www.brookings.edu/opinions/2003/03middleeast_taspinar.aspx, accessed 20 July 2011.

19. http://www.meforum.org/696/eurabia-europes-future, accessed 20 July 2011.

20. http://www.meforum.org/2660/can-jihadis-be-rehabilitated, accessed 20 July 2011.

JIM DENISON

James C. Denison, Ph.D., is a cultural apologist, building a bridge between faith and culture by engaging contemporary issues with biblical truth. He founded the Denison Forum on Truth and Culture in February 2009.

Having lived and traveled widely in the Muslim world, Dr. Denison has wide expertise on the subject of Islam. He has also taught world religions for 25 years with four seminaries. He has spoken in China, Cuba, Brazil, Australia, Europe, Israel, Greece, Egypt, Bangladesh and Turkey and served as a shortterm missionary to East Malaysia, in Southeast Asia. He also leads frequent study tours in Israel, Greece, and Europe.

Dr. Denison currently serves on the board of the Baylor Health Care System and as chair of the advisory Board for Dallas Baptist University. He teaches Ph.D. seminars and graduate-level classes for Dallas Baptist University and serves as a teaching fellow for the B. H. Carroll Theological Institute. He has taught on the faculty of Southwestern Baptist Theological Seminary and at McAfee School of Theology, and has served on the boards of Dallas Baptist University, George W. Truett Theological Seminary and the Center for Christian Ethics at Baylor University.

Prior to founding the Forum, Dr. Denison was senior pastor of Park Cities Baptist Church, a 10,000-member congregation in Dallas, Texas. He also pastored churches in Midland and Mansfield, Texas and in Atlanta, Georgia. He earned his Ph.D. in Philosophy of Religion and Master of Divinity from Southwestern Baptist Theological Seminary and received a Doctor of Divinity degree from Dallas Baptist University.

He is the author of six books:

- *Wrestling with God: How Can I Love a God I'm Not Sure I Can Trust?*
- *The Bible–You Can Believe It: Biblical Authority in the Twenty-First Century*
- *The Myth and the Manger*
- *Life on the Brick Pile: Answers to Suffering from the Letters of Revelation*
- *Seven Crucial Questions About the Bible*
- *It's Your Mission: The Church's Responsibility to the Least of These*

Dr. Denison writes a daily cultural commentary available at www.denisonforum.org. His commentary is distributed around the world to more than 19,000 subscribers. He writes for The Dallas Morning News, contributing weekly to the "Texas Faith Forum."

His wife, Janet, is an author and speaker (www.janetdenison.com). They live in Dallas and are the parents of two sons: Ryan, a ministry student at Truett Seminary, and Craig, a ministry student at Dallas Baptist University.

ENDORSEMENTS

"A must read if you desire to understand the times in which we live as Christians. Each generation of Christians have unique "times" they must deal with in proclaiming the love of Christ. Jim clearly set the stage for our generation related to the proclamation of the gospel in the context of the greatest religious opportunity in the history of the Church."

John Maisel, Founder and Chairman Emeritus
East-West Ministries International

"For over 25 years I have known Jim Denison to be a world-class scholar with a keen eye on global affairs and the human condition. He provides a timely overview of Islam and the dangers of radical belief while pointing the way toward mutual respect, understanding, and peace among people of differing worldviews. Denison's research, written from philosophical, theological, and biblical perspectives, brings much needed clarity to the work of anyone interested in sharing the love of Jesus in tangible ways."

Albert L. Reyes, DMin, PhD
President, Buckner International

"We all know the questions: Why did 9-11 happen? Can we win the war on terror? Is radical Islam a real threat to the American way of life? How can we distinguish between real concerns regarding the Islamic faith and right-wing hype?

In this new work, Jim Denison does what he does best – tackles the hard questions with an open mind, courage, in-depth research, and a kind heart. If you have read any other books concerning radical Islam, you must counterbalance their arguments and enhance your understanding of the issues with Denison's reasoned approach. Denison brings the "word" for which we've all been waiting."

Howard K. Batson, Ph.D.
Pastor, First Baptist Church of Amarillo, Texas

Past Endorsements:

"Scholar/Pastor James Denison tackles life's ultimate questions head-on—biblical authority, evil and suffering, prayer and providence, faith and reason, and the fate of the unevangelized—with an approach that is both erudite and down-to-earth."

Russell H. Dilday
Chancellor, B. H. Carroll Theological Institute
Arlington, TX

"*Wrestling with God* is an excellent book for anyone struggling with trusting God. With humility and honesty, wisdom and compassion, Jim Denison's words will help us embrace the scarred hand of our powerful Creator and loving Redeemer."

Gary Cook
President, Dallas Baptist University

"As a father who has buried one child and gone through a brain tumor with another, I find that Jim Denison raises many of my own questions in *Wrestling with God*—and then answers them out of the biblical reality that grace always emerges out of suffering."

Ronald W. Scates
Senior Pastor, Highland Park Presbyterian Church
Dallas, TX

"*Wrestling with God* is a must-read for any Christian who has struggled with difficult questions regarding his or her faith in God, offering tremendous insight into how we can have a deeper relationship with God."

Joel T. Allison
President and CEO,
Baylor Health Care System